Preface

Despite all the criticism of GDP as a metric to assess the economic performance, GDP has remained the sole financial magic number since several decades, which is awaited by many at the end of every quarter and at the end of every year.

GDP acts as a report card of the prevailing government's economic performance. An average citizen takes the latest GDP growth rate number and compare it against the previous period number. If the latest number is better than the number in the prior period, then we assume that government's economic performance is satisfactory. But citing the sheer economic significance attached to GDP, an average citizen needs to expand one's horizons and understand this term named, GDP, in a better way.

There is an interesting economic history associated with GDP - how it was conceptualized, adopted and evolved over time. There are various relative metrics associated with GDP, which is used to compare the country's economic standing vis-a-vis other countries.

There is something called "business cycle", which comprises multiple phases or stages- expansion, peak, contraction, and trough. Each such stage affects GDP differently and each such stage may last more than a year.

There are various inputs to GDP - labour, capital and productivity/technological advancements. Each such input has a different weightage in different countries.

There are various driving forces behind the GDP. We need to know all these in a detailed way. It is also quite interesting to know how GDP growth rate usually get impacted during major economic crisis (by learning from past economic crisis).

Though we understand the utility of GDP, but it is imperative to understand the dark side of GDP as well. GDP uses the organised sector data to measure growth in the unorganised sector also and assumes that both the sectors are growing at the same rate. This may lead to misleading economic report card for a country where unorganised sectors contribution to GDP is higher (e.g. Emerging markets such as India). There are various other unfavourable arguments against GDP that we all must know.

There are various alternatives to GDP suggested by eminent economists such as Fordham Index of Social Health (FISH), Genuine Progress Indicator (GPI), Human Development Index (HDI) and Happy Planet Index (HPI). We need to analyse each such alternatives.

There are various myths associated with GDP. One popular myth is – comparing the market capitalisation of trillion-dollar club companies - Apple or Microsoft or Google/Alphabet with the GDP of a country. If market capitalisation exceeds the GDP, then we assume that company has set some important economic milestone. But logically, such comparison is utterly irrational comparison.

I hope you would find this book informative and useful.

ORGANIZATION OF THE BOOK

The book has been organized into six chapters. A brief description of each of the chapters are as follows:

Chapter 1: GDP – An overview

Provides a detailed overview of GDP, its significance and why it is widely used across the world. It further provides an overview of GDP growth rate and its economic significance. It also touches upon the geopolitical history of GDP, how it evolved and how it got adopted by several countries.

Chapter 2: GDP – Its Components and How it varies across the world

Presents a detailed overview of key components of GDP by analysing major countries and how GDP varies across the different countries.

Chapter 3: Business Cycles – How it affects the GDP and Markets

Presents a detailed overview of the impact of business cycle on Equity markets, Bond Markets and FX Markets. It also touches upon the business cycle, its relationship with GDP growth rate and how long does each business cycle last.

Chapter 4: GDP growth – Key Input factors & Its Percentage Contribution

Presents a detailed overview of key factors of GDP Growth– labour, capital and productivity. It also provides details on how these factors changes across different regions across the world.

Chapter 5: GDP Growth – Key Driving forces and determinants of higher Growth

It provides a detail about key driving forces and determinants of higher economic growth. There is a study about high income, medium income and low-income countries.

Chapter 6: GDP growth during Unusual Circumstances

Presents a holistic overview of GDP growth rate performance during past economic crisis – World war-II, Nepal post-earthquake economic growth, 1957 Asian Flu Pandemic.

Chapter 7: GDP – Its Limitations and its alternatives

It describes the limitations of using GDP to measure the economic development of a country. It also describes about some emerging alternatives of GDP such as FISH, GPI, HDI and HPI.

Chapter 8: GDP – Myths Associated with it

It describes the common myths associated with GDP such as GDP is equivalent to company's revenue. Debt to GDP is better measure compared to Debt to government revenue.

Chapter-1

GDP – An Overview

- What is GDP?
- Economic size across the world
- Why GDP is important?
- What is GDP growth rate and Why it is important?
- Political history of GDP

What is GDP?

The term "GDP" has now gone mainstream. It is no longer confined to be used by a handful of economists or investment professionals. GDP has started being widely used by mainstream media (i.e. non-business media). The popularity of this 3-letter magic word can be fathomed by the fact that the political opponents in developed or developing or under-developed countries find themselves at ease with using this term to target the ruling government (whenever GDP growth rate drops).

A large section of people do have a decent level of awareness that GDP is all about economy of the country. Higher the value, the better the country's prospects are. Given the national importance associated with the GDP, we all need to understand it in a better way.

So, what GDP really is?

Gross Domestic Product ("GDP") is one of the most common economic barometers across the world to measure the size of a country's economy. It measures the monetary value (in dollar terms) of all goods and services produced over a specific measurement period. The measurement period is usually quarterly and at the end of the fourth quarter, quarterly GDP is reported as annualised growth rate (i.e. at the end of 4 quarters the quarterly growth rate is annualised).

If we compare a country's GDP with a company financial statement, then GDP is akin to company's annual cashflow. At times, we mistook GDP as annual revenue of the country, but it is not equivalent to the annual revenue of the company.

Country's annual revenue is its revenue receipts, which is far less than the country's GDP. Higher the GDP figure (in USD denomination), the larger is the size of the country's economy. Larger the size of the country's economy, the bigger is the clout of that country in the global trade.

GDP can be measured at current prices or at constant prices. GDP at current prices does not account for inflation while computing the GDP final value. GDP at current price is also known as nominal GDP. GDP at constant price accounts for the inflation.

GDP uses a "Base Year" and a "Price level" for that base year. The price level or price index or GDP deflator of base year is used to adjust nominal GDP to arrive at the real GDP. The Real GDP is, thus, adjusted for the inflation rate. The GDP deflator measures the average prices of all finished goods and services produced within a nation's borders over time.

The Gross Domestic Product, that is compared across different countries are of two kinds-

- Nominal
- Purchasing power parity (PPP)

GDP-Nominal is the total size of the economy (in USD terms, usually). It is unadjusted for the inflation.

GDP-PPP is the total size of the country's economy, normalized for local price variations in a country. GDP-PPP is usually higher than the GDP-nominal for majority of the countries. This suggests that the local purchasing power (within the territories of the country's borders) of most of the country's currency is stronger. i.e. with the same $1 money converted into local currency terms, one can buy more goods in a country where the GDP-PPP is higher.

But across the world, economists use the GDP-nominal (in USD terms) for comparing the size of the country's economy.

Economic Size across the world

Below are the top 10 largest economies in the world (as of Dec 2019):

United States: (GDP-Nominal: $20.49 trillion)
China: (GDP-Nominal: $13.4 trillion)
Japan: (GDP-Nominal: $4.97 trillion)
Germany: (GDP-Nominal: $4.00 trillion)
UK: (GDP-Nominal: $2.83 trillion)
France: (GDP-Nominal: $2.78 trillion)
India: (GDP-Nominal: $2.72 trillion)
Italy: (GDP-Nominal: $2.07 trillion)
Brazil: (GDP-Nominal: $1.87 trillion)
Canada: (GDP-Nominal: $1.71 trillion)

Global GDP stands at $92 trillion. It is almost 4 times the size of US economy.

The global economy is quite opaque and the distribution of size of the economy is not uniform across the world. Some countries have excessively larger economy while others are endowed with a very smaller sized economy. The nominal GDP of the top 10 economies adds up to about 66% of the world's economy, while the top 20 economies contribute almost 79% to the world's economy. ⬚ The remaining 173 countries together constitute less than one-fourth to the world's economy.

So, why do some countries have an excessively larger economy and some countries are so small?

It is because of some countries have had a long growth stories because of their favourable economic policies. These countries grew its economy so much year after year for many decades and turned their countries into an economic behemoth.

Some countries lag others because of the following factors-

Higher Debt level – Because of higher debt, country must spend a large portion of the revenue (collected as taxes) on debt repayment and interest payment. They are left with inadequate money to spend on the development projects.

Difficult landscapes and extreme weather conditions – Because of difficult landscapes and extreme weather conditions (very hot or constant typhoon, etc.), it is very hard to get the development done.

Political leadership – Keeping other factors as constant, political leadership in a country plays a very important role in a country's development.

Due to combined effects of all the above factors, many countries remain in a vicious cycle of poverty. Economy does not perform at its optimal level. It results in lower personal income for its residents. Because of which, most People do not get an access to food and safe drinking water. Hunger and poor sanitation are the after-effects of such situations. It results in disease, malnutrition and death. It affects the country's workforce. Country gets a depleted and less-productive workforce. This adversely impacts the overall economy further.

Thus, this cycle goes on.

Why GDP is so important?

We went through the term GDP in the above section, now we will try to understand- why GDP is so important and how different are its two variants – GDP-nominal and GDP-PPP.

We already know that GDP measures the size of the economy. Larger the size, larger the country's clout in the global trade. The size of economy acts a cushion for the country to take additional risks to grow the country's economy even further. GDP is also used as a relative figure to measure so many other important dimensions of country's economy. Those dimensions may be immaterial if they are analysed on a standalone basis (without measuring it relative to GDP).

Some of those important dimensions of economy, which are normally used in respect to GDP (nominal), not on a standalone basis are:

1. Country's total Debt
2. Country's Tax Revenue
3. Country's Annual Income
4. Country's Current Account Balance

1. Country's total Debt

Total Debt is the capital mobilised by state and federal government through other lending countries or organisations. It is usually measured as Total Debt/GDP ratio.
e.g. A XYZ Country's debt is $500 billion but its GDP is $5 trillion then Country's total Debt/GDP = 0.5/5 = 0.1 = 10%.

On an absolute level, debt figure of $500 billion appears to a be a very large amount. But if we measure it in terms of Debt/GDP (as it is done usually by global rating agencies) then it is just 10% of its economy's size. So, the total debt's measurement with respect to GDP tells us about the financial risk of that country with respect to its economy's size. If country's economic size (i.e. GDP) is considerably higher than total debt level, then it lessens the economic risk for that country. This is also known as financial leverage of the country.

Few examples of countries and its Debt/GDP ratio:
Japan - 237%
US - 106%
France - 99%
Brazil - 90%
Pakistan - 77%
India - 69%

Larger the size of the economy (i.e. GDP), larger the absolute debt level, a country can afford to have without hurting the sovereign credit rating the country.

But there is a caveat to it as well.

As per rule of thumb of the IMF, Risk premium increases by 4 bps (basis points) for every percentage of the debt to GDP ratio above 60%. Let's compute India's average cost of debt by incorporating the IMF assumptions about risk premium for cost of debt:

India, with a debt-to-GDP ratio of approximately 70%, i.e. almost 10% above the 60% threshold set by IMF (for increase in risk premium), the predicted risk premium should be 40 bps. With a risk-free rate i.e. 10 Y local currency (i.e. INR) government bonds close to 6.1% (as of May 2, 2020), the marginal cost of additional debt = 6.1% + 40 bps = 6.5%.

With a debt level at 70% of GDP, total interest expenses roughly amount to 4.55% (= 6.5*0.70) of GDP. This figure of 4.55% reveals that the country must grow by at least 4.55% in order to have enough tax revenue to pay the interest rate annually to its creditor countries and organisations. Failed to do so, may result in refinancing the debt through additional new debts. This becomes a vicious debt cycle for many countries.

2. Country's Tax Revenue

Tax Revenue is the combination of direct and indirect taxes that is imposed by federal or state government on income, goods or services. The accumulated annual tax revenue at country level is usually measured as Tax Revenue/GDP ratio.

e.g. Country's Revenue is $500 billion but its GDP is $2.5 trillion then Country's tax revenue/GDP = 0.5/2.5 = 0.2 = 20%.

On an absolute level, the tax revenue figure of $500 billion appears to be a too large amount. But if we measure it in terms of Tax revenue/GDP (as it is done usually by global rating agencies) then it is just 20% of its economy's size.

Larger the economy's size (i.e. GDP), the larger figure of tax revenue is expected from that country. If the tax revenue is quite low with respect to its economy's size, then tax revenue may not be sufficient for the government to meet its spending needs. Government may have to resort to other avenues for meeting the shortfall in tax revenue collection.

This ratio is also one of the important determinants of sovereign credit rating. Few examples of countries and its tax revenue/GDP ratio:

Norway	- 55%
Finland	- 54%
Denmark	- 51%
Sweden	- 50%
France	- 48%
Germany	- 44%
UK	- 34%
China	- 20%
US	- 27%
India	- 11%

Most of the Nordic countries (Norway, Finland, Denmark and Sweden) have a higher tax revenue/GDP ratio because of the higher taxation rate in these regions. Individual tax rate (direct tax) in these countries range between 45-55%, one of the highest rates in the world. Most of Nordic countries are ranked amongst the best in the world on most of the prosperity indices – HDI index, Happiness Index.

OECD countries have average tax-to-GDP ratio of 34%.

India is amongst the lowest taxed countries in the world. That could be one of the root cause of the most of malaise in the country.

Below bar-chart details the breakdown of the tax-to-GDP in terms of its revenue source for the Nordic countries (Denmark, Norway & Sweden) and United States.

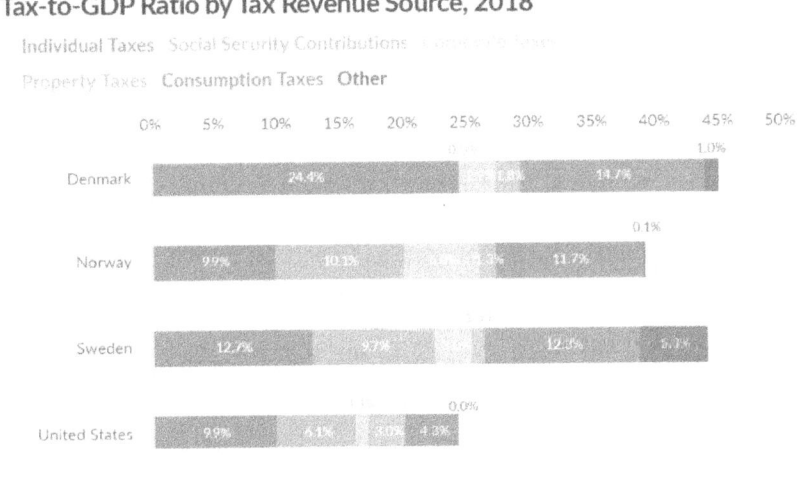

Tax-to-GDP Ratio by Tax Revenue Source, 2018

Individual Taxes   Social Security Contributions
Property Taxes   Consumption Taxes   Other

Note: U.S. payroll taxes are defined as social security contributions in this graph.
Source: OECD, "Global Revenue Statistics Database"

For Nordic countries, Individual and Social security combined (20-25%) is the biggest contributor to overall tax revenue collection. Second biggest contributor is Consumption tax (indirect tax). Its contribution to total tax revenue is around 11-15%. Corporate tax's share in overall tax revenue quite less, around 3-6%.

For US, Individual and Social security combined (~16%) is the biggest contributor to overall tax revenue collection. Second biggest contributor is Consumption tax (~4%). Corporate tax's share in overall tax revenue is quite less (~3%).

One of the major differences between Nordic countries and US is the contribution of Individual and Social security combined in Nordic countries' GDP is almost 50% more than what is prevailing in US. Contribution of Consumption tax in Nordic countries' GDP is almost 3 times the US consumption tax contribution level.

3.   Country's Annual Income

Annual Income of the country is usually measured as GDP/Total Population. Also, known as GDP per capita.

e.g. India's Population is 1.3 Billion, but its GDP is $2.7 trillion then India's GDP per capita = $2700/1.3 = $2077 per annum.

On an absolute level, GDP figure of $2.7 trillion appears to be a quite a large amount. But if we measure the income in terms of GDP per capita (as it is done usually by global rating agencies) then it is just $2077 per annum. i.e. $173 per month.

GDP per capita is a common measure of level of affluence of a country. Top 10 countries (plus United States) in terms of Annual GDP per capita are (as per World Bank, 2018):

Qatar:	$126,898
Macao:	$123,892
Luxembourg:	$113,337
Singapore:	$101, 531
Ireland:	$83,203
Brunei:	$80,920
UAE:	$75,075
Kuwait:	$72,897.6
Cayman Islands:	$72,607.6
Switzerland:	$68,060
United States:	$62,795

Some of the middle-east countries and tax-haven nations such Qatar, Kuwait, UAE, Macao, Luxembourg and Caymans Islands are among top 10 richest countries (as measured by GDP per capita).

Income level of a country can further be split into its age-group. Below bar-chart, captures the average income of US residents at different age-group level.

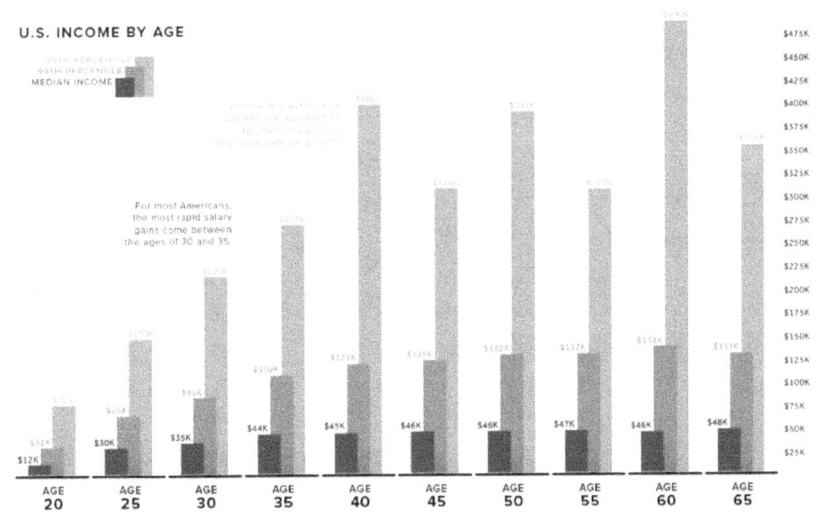

Source: Visual Capitalist

There are two commonly held beliefs around the people's income and their age (which may differ slightly for different countries):

1) Earning trajectory of an individual is determined once a person reaches 35+ year age-group
2) An Individual's Income is directly correlated with his/her age. i.e. higher the age, higher the individual's average income.

By looking at the above bar-chart, both above two common beliefs appear to be true for United States.

4. Country's Current Account Balance

The current account balance (Surplus or deficit) is a measurement of a country's trade. It is measured as the value of the goods and services that a country exports minus the value of the goods and services it exports to other countries. Surplus is a situation when country's "exports" is greater than its "imports". While, deficit is a situation when country's "imports" is greater than its "exports".

For a comparison with other countries, Deficit or Surplus is represented as Current account Surplus or Deficit/GDP ratio. e.g. Country's current account deficit is $100 billion but its GDP is $2.5 trillion then Country's current account deficit/GDP = 0.1/2.5 = 0.04 = 4%.

On an absolute level, current account deficit figure of $100 billion appears to be a too large amount. But if we measure it in terms of current account deficit/GDP (as it is done usually by global rating agencies) then it is just 4% of its economy's size.

The Current account surplus or deficit-to-GDP ratio is also one of the important determinants of sovereign credit rating and the exchange rate of the country.

Few examples of countries and its current account balance as % of GDP for a random year (positive value below indicates a surplus and negative value indicates a deficit):

United States: -2.3%
Brazil: -2.7%
India: -2.1%
Taiwan: 11.6%
Singapore: 16.9%

The current account deficit or surplus situation are common phenomenon in global trades. A country might be running a surplus with few countries, but it might be in deficit with its other trading partner countries. But still country might be able turn its overall trade at country level into surplus.

A country's surplus is other country's deficit. So, at overall worldwide level, surplus countries' trade is equal to deficit countries' trade. But the distribution of surplus size and deficit size varies as the time passes.

Below bar-chart tells us how the surplus size of countries is changing with the corresponding change in the share of deficit size of other countries.

Below chart has an actual data for 2002-2018 and projected data for 2018-2024.

Figure 1 Global current balances for select country aggregates

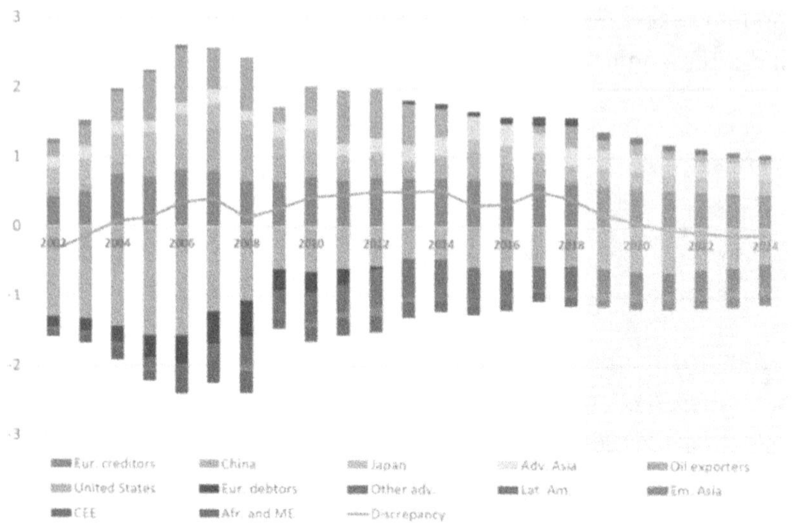
3
2
1
0
-1
-2
-3
2002
2004
2006
2008
2010
2012
2014
2016
2018
2020
2022
2024
Eur. creditors
China
Japan
Adv. Asia
Oil exporters
United States
Eur. debtors
Other adv.
Lat. Am.
Em. Asia
CEE
Afr. and ME
Discrepancy

Source: IMF

United States had been a dominant consumer of the global trade and hence had run a larger deficit economy (more than 1% of GDP) from 2002-2008. This deficit level has been reducing after global financial crisis in 2008. It is close to 0.5% of GDP since past few years and forecasted to remain at this level till 2024.

On the other hand, China had been a dominant producer of the global trade and hence had run a larger surplus economy (increased its surplus size from 2002-2008). The surplus size of China has been decreasing since 2008. While surplus size has remained almost unchanged for the oil exporting nations and Japan.

What is GDP Growth Rate?

In the above section, we went through the broader term named "GDP". Now, we will go through a term named – "GDP Growth Rate".

There is a stark difference between the term GDP and GDP Growth Rate. Now-a-days GDP is often mistakenly used to denote the GDP Growth rate (and vice-versa) within political discourse and by non-business media.

In the recent time, "GDP" and "GDP growth rate" are no longer confined to the financial lexicon. For a Government, a better GDP growth rate provides a reason to brag about the country's economic accomplishments.

For political opponents, a not-so-good GDP growth rate number, gives some ammunitions to opposition party to attack the ruling government over its not-so-effective economic policies (which resulted in lower GDP growth rate number).

GDP Growth rate is Year-On-Year percentage change of GDP. It is usually computed 4 times a year - after completion of each quarter, e.g. Jan-March, April-June, July-Sep and Oct-Dec. Then after the end of 4th quarter, the figure is annualized to arrive at the annual GDP growth rate figure.

Though financial year convention varies between different countries. For many countries, it is Jan-Dec but for some countries, it is April-March.

e.g. if GDP continues to grow at 0.96% for four quarters it would have grown at 3.80% annual rate. [(1.0096 x 1.0096 x 1.0096 x 1.0096)-1].

When a quarterly GDP rate is published by government agency, it reports the figure in annualised term (i.e. 3.8%) not in quarterly growth term (0.96%).

The GDP Growth rate are presented in two ways:

- Real GDP growth rate
- Nominal GDP growth rate

Nominal GDP growth rate is not adjusted for inflation rate while real GDP growth rate is adjusted for inflation rate.

Usually, GDP is reported as "nominal" GDP. But GDP growth rate is reported as "Real" GDP growth rate.

Nominal GDP and GDP growth rate for top 10 global economies

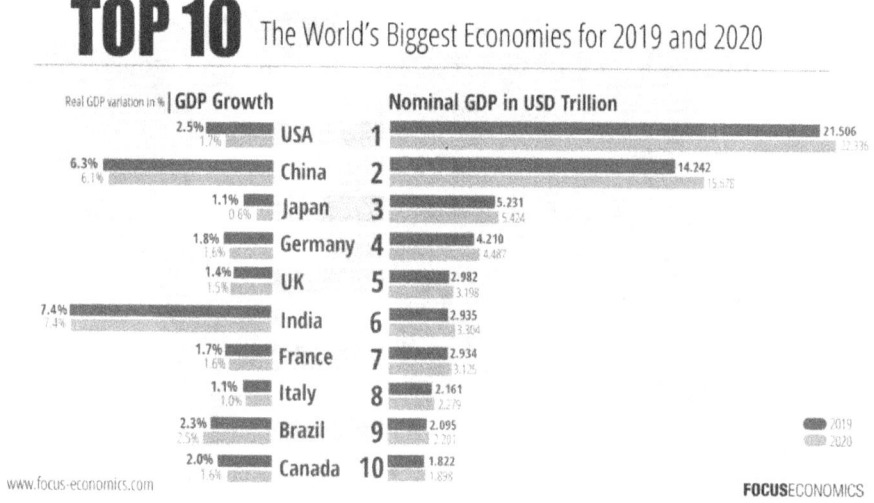

Source: Focus-Economics

Economy size-wise United States is the largest economies in the world, having nominal GDP of around $22 trillion. China is the second largest economy with nominal GDP of around $15 trillion. India is placed at 6th position with a nominal GDP at $3 trillion.

Annual GDP growth rate-wise, India is fasted growing large economy at 7% annual GDP growth. China is second fastest growing large economy at 6%. US annual GDP growth rate is quite dismal at 1.7% growth rate.

Developed countries usually have lower GDP growth rate compared to their emerging or developing countries counterparts because of the larger size of developed countries' economy. While developing countries' economy size is relatively smaller, it usually has a greater potential to grow further (i.e. low base effect).

Why is GDP growth rate so important?

1. GDP growth rate gives an outlook for revenue (tax collections) growth for the Government. It provides a base for the government to plan its annual budget.
2. A higher GDP growth rate signals a good revenue growth for the corporates.
3. For Salaried class, it acts as an impetus for the wage growth.
4. If GDP growth rate falls below the borrowing rate of a country, then it is likely to affect the sovereign credit rating of the country. It also results in further borrowing becoming costlier for the government.
5. It is used by central bank to gauge the economic cycle of the economy. If GDP growth is too high and above its potential, then interest rate is recommended to move up else it is recommended to cut down.
6. When GDP growth rate is positive and higher than same quarter last year, the economy is generally thought to be doing well. A weak growth signals that the economy is not doing well.
7. If nominal GDP is less than same quarter last year, then GDP growth is negative for that quarter. It usually represents the falling incomes, lower consumption and higher employment rate (or job-loss). The economy is in recession when there are two consecutive quarters of negative GDP growth.

8.   For common man, a lower GDP translates into a proportionate decline in per capita income. Further, for economy where inequality (distribution of wealth) is higher, it is very likely that the poor will suffer more from the drop in the GDP growth rate than the rich.

9.   In 1962, Arthur Okun, staff economist for U.S. President John F. Kennedy's Council of Economic Advisers, coins **Okun's Law**. As per this law, for every 3-point rise in GDP, unemployment will fall 1 percentage point. The theory guides US monetary policy.

Political history of GDP

Though warfare has often given a rise to humanitarian crisis in the world. But warfare also has some other aspects to it. Many new technologies that end up being an integral part of the civilian's life, have been spurred by the demands of conflicts and funded by the military.

Warfare has given an impetus to many inventions – ranging from Internet, Radar, and electronic computers. All these inventions, done during the war or severe political conflicts, give an edge to the inventing countries over its adversaries.

GDP is also one of the many inventions that came out from the Warfare. There were a series of refinement in the approach to compute the GDP or national income & expense since its first adoption in 1665. During its initial adoption, it was not known as GDP though.

We will go through the below 7 difference periods of evolution of GDP since 17th Century-

- 17th Century - William Petty
- 18th Century - Jacques Necker
- First half of 20th Century - Maynard Keynes
- First half of 20th Century - Simon Kuznets
- Second Half of 20th Century - Milton Friedman
- Post WWII - Peacetime uses of GDP
- Second half of 20th Century - Okun's Law

17th Century - William Petty

In 1665 (During Second Anglo-Dutch War - 1665 to 1667), a British scientist and Government official, William Petty proposed the idea of "political arithmetic" i.e. the notion that the rulers should base their political decisions on numbers and statistics. He created a national account with estimates of the income & expenditure, population, land and other assets of England and Wales.

Before that for many centuries, no government was convinced that numbers and statistic mattered. William Petty produced estimates of the income and expenditure. It includes various components such as population (value of people), land, ships, personal estates & housing and other assets of England and Wales.

His aim was to measure the total wealth of the economy in order to assess the country's resources with regards to its ability to fight a conflict and finance it through taxes. Thus, national account system was born, which few centuries later evolved into GDP.

Petty wanted to prove two things – one, country could bear a higher tax burden and economy is strong enough to fight against its powerful neighbours, Holland and France. In order to keep proper records of income and expense at country level, Petty applied the concept of double-entry bookkeeping, a significant accounting innovation during those times.

For England, a consolidated national income statistic enabled the government to calculate the scope for an increased output and tax revenues, a crucial information for the English government. It helped them plan its frequent wars with France appropriately.

18th Century - Jacques Necker

Britain's powerful neighbour, France did have access to such accounting information. It took France almost a century (somewhere at the end of 18th century) to come up with a similar national income and expense accounting concept what England had been using since the end of 17th century.

French King Louis XVI's finance minister, Jacques Necker, came up with a famous "compte rendu au roi," or "Financial Summary for the King" report. It captured the details about the strength of the French economy. This information assured French king to raise new loans.

By 18th century the concept of "national income" was seemingly clear enough for many countries, but there was no consensus among the statistical pioneers on the actual measurement. They were quite divided on what to include and what to exclude while doing the national income measurement. But still the objective of this measurement was primarily to finance warfare through the available resources.

First half of 20th Century - Maynard Keynes

During WWII, British economist John Maynard Keynes, who was working with Bank of England (UK treasury), published an essay on "How to Pay for the War" in 1939. Keynes wanted to have a reliable statistic available to him for calculating - what the British economy could produce with the available resources. During those warfare periods, he wanted to be able to understand:

- What would be left over for people to consume — and how much their living standards would get impacted because of that.
- How much was produced by individual industries, including what materials they used.

In principle, the war might be funded by following ways—

- Using the past savings of the nation
- Using the current taxes
- Using borrowing (abroad or domestically)
- Through the higher inflation

In 1939, John Maynard Keynes identified that even in wartime there were choices. The efficiency of capital mobilisation for funding the war efforts and the distribution of funding burdens on workers, lenders, and future generations would depend on the funding method chosen.

The impulse of the UK government at the start of the WWII had been to regulate the markets and the control the supply. In order to achieve this, Keynes proposed to control the demand by using government taxes and compulsory savings. One of the problems Keynes identified was that the wartime spending would overwhelm the normal business cycle and cause over-heating i.e. inflationary pressure will come into the economy.

Keynes helped organise the first major UK National Accounts. He accepted that post-war economic stabilisation would become a major problem as the aggregate demand would fall sharply after the war. It was unclear whether there would be a labour shortage or a shortage of consumption after the war. He also thought about how to activate the economic stabilisation tools of fiscal and monetary policy after the end of the war, in the peacetime periods with a stabilised demand.

First half of 20th Century - Simon Kuznets

In 1937, Simon Kuznets, an economist at the US National Bureau of Economic Research, presented the original formulation of GDP in his report to the U.S. Congress, "**National Income, 1929-35**."

Simon Kuznets advocated to capture all economic production by individuals, companies, and the government in a single measure, which should rise in good times and fall in bad. Thus, the modern GDP was born.

Kuznets found that Keynes' predictions, though, seemingly accurate in short-run, does not hold true in long term. In his 1942 research paper, "Uses of National Income in Peace and War", published by the National Bureau of Economic Research, Kuznets showed that the Absolute Income Hypothesis (as espoused by Keynes) gives inaccurate predictions in the long run. Keynes had predicted that as aggregate income increases, so will marginal savings. Kuznets used new data to show that, over a longer span of time (1870s – 1940s) the savings ratio remained constant, despite large changes in income.

Second Half of 20th Century - Milton Friedman

Later, another US economist Milton Friedman, in his "permanent income" hypothesis found out that person's consumption at a point in time is determined not just by their current income but also by their expected income in future years—their "permanent income". In its simplest form, the hypothesis states that changes in the permanent income, rather than changes in the temporary income, drive the changes in a consumer's consumption patterns. A worker will save only if his or her current income is higher than the expected income (i.e. permanent income), in order to guard against future declines in the income.

Keynes argued that fiscal policy by the government can help overcome recessions by propping up aggregate demand. Strategic government spending could spur consumption & investment and help alleviate unemployment. But Friedman argued that Keynesian economics has facilitated the short-sighted government to run the fiscal deficits and accumulate the massive levels of government debt, which is unsustainable in the long run.

Friedman opposed many of theories espoused by the Keynesian economists in the post-War period. He advocated the deregulation in major segments of the economy, calling for a return to the free market theory. He challenged contemporary notions of deficit spending and suggested that, in the long run, expansionary fiscal policy is unsustainable.

Friedman argued for free trade, smaller government and a slow, steady increase of the money supply in a growing economy. His emphasis on monetary policy and the quantity theory of money became known as "monetarism".

In 1944, following the Bretton Woods conference that established international financial institutions such as the World Bank and the International Monetary Fund, GDP becomes the standard tool for sizing up a country's economy and for measuring the annual economic performance of a country.

Post WWII - Peacetime uses of GDP

In 1946, the peacetime development of GDP statistics started taking its shape. A Committee of Statistical Experts, in New York, was tasked to come up with recommendations for collecting national statistics on behalf of the UN. Further, UN helped in setting an international standard of measurement (now known as "System of National Accounts"-SNA).

Post-World War II, the reconstruction of Western Europe was one of the greatest economic policy and foreign policy successes of this century. "Folk wisdom" assigns a major role in successful reconstruction to the Marshall Plan: the program that transferred some $13 billion to Europe in the years 1948-51.

The brainchild of U.S. Secretary of State George C. Marshall, for whom it was named, it was crafted as a four-year plan to reconstruct cities, industries and infrastructure heavily damaged during the war and to remove trade barriers between European neighbours – as well as foster commerce between those countries and the United States.

The transfer represented approximately 2 per cent of U.S. GDP and roughly the same share of the collective GDP of the recipient countries.

President Harry Truman signed the Marshall Plan on April 3, 1948, and aid was distributed to 16 European nations, including Britain, France, Belgium, the Netherlands, West Germany and Norway. Marshall Plan adopted GDP as metric to collect the data needed to distribute the aid to European economies.

The recipients got the aid on a per capita basis, with larger amounts given to major industrial powers, such as West Germany, France and Great Britain. This was based on the belief of Marshall and his advisors that recovery in these larger nations was essential to overall European recovery. The largest recipient of Marshall Plan money was the United Kingdom (receiving about 26% of the total), followed by France (18%) and West Germany (11%).

Second half of 20th Century - Okun's Law

In 1962, Arthur Okun, staff economist for U.S. President John F. Kennedy's Council of Economic Advisers, coins Okun's Law. As per this law, for every 3-point rise in GDP, unemployment will fall 1 percentage point. The theory guides monetary policy: Keep growing the economy and everything will be just fine.

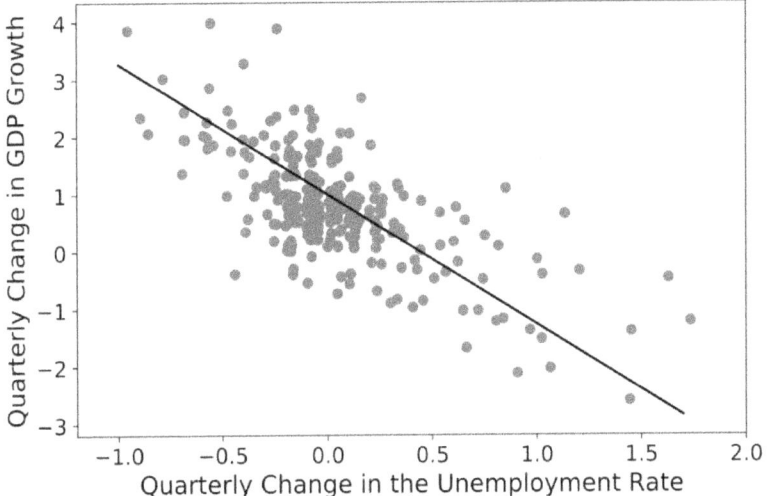

Chapter-2

GDP – Its Computation, Components and how it varies across the world

- Different ways of GDP computation
- GDP – Its Key components
- Analysis of Major countries and its GDP
- How business cycle affects the GDP
- How long does each business cycle last?

Different ways of GDP computation

Before understanding the key components of GDP, let's understand how GDP is usually computed. GDP can be computed using below 3 approaches:

- Output Approach
- Expenditure approach
- Income Approach

Output Approach

The output approach is also called "net product" or "value added" method. This method consists of three stages:
- Estimating the gross value of domestic output;
- Determining the intermediate consumption, i.e., the cost of material, supplies, and services used to produce final goods or services;
- Deducting intermediate consumption from gross value to obtain the net value of domestic output.

Net value added = Gross value of output – Value of intermediate consumption.
Where, Gross value of output = Value of the total sales of goods and services + Value of changes in the inventories.

Expenditure approach

The most well-known approach to calculating GDP, the expenditure approach is characterized by the following formula:

GDP = C + I + G + (X-M)

Where C is the level of consumption of goods and services, I is gross investment, G is government purchases, X is exports, and M is imports.

Income Approach

According to the income approach, GDP can be computed by finding total national income (TNI) and then adjusting it for sales taxes (T), depreciation (D), and net foreign factor income (F).

Thus, we can use the following formula:

GDP = TNI + T + D + F

Income and Expenditure approach both computes the monetary value of all final goods & services produced in an economy over a period of time.

GDP – Its key components

Let's now understand the key components of GDP from the perspective of Expenditure Approach (as you read in earlier section).

Below are four key components of GDP in a country. Characteristics of each country's economy is such that one of the below four components may contribute more than the other remaining components (i.e. net exports components may be the largest contributor to overall GDP for a certain country; but for others personal consumption may be the largest contributor to overall GDP.

- Personal Consumption (By retail consumers) - C
- Business Investment (By Corporates) - I
- Expenses (By Government) - G
- Net Exports (at country level) - NX

The formula to calculate the components of GDP is Y = C + I + G + NX

Personal consumption

It broadly includes:

- Durable goods (Items with lifespan greater than 3 years) – e.g. cars, furniture, large appliances.

- Non-durable goods (Items with lesser lifespan) – e.g. clothing, food, fuel.
- Services – e.g. banking, health care, education. Services are paid help, or information. Most are non-tangible.

If people keep spending same amount of money every year then it won't help the growth of the economy. So, it is very imperative that this personal consumption keeps rising every year.

Let's see what are those determinants which affects the growth in Personal Consumption:

- Income or wage growth (Y-O-Y)
  An economic environment, in which sustainable level of wage growth is happening, results in higher GDP growth, keeping other parameters constant.

- Level of accumulated wealth
  A family with higher accumulated wealth is expected to do more spending on consumptions, keeping other parameters constant.

- Expectations about the level and riskiness of future income or wealth
  If the future economic situation (which dictates the employment situations) is expected to remain stable, then consumer is inclined to keep its consumption level same or increase it.

- Prevailing Interest rates
  A consumer will not think twice to consume more than its capacity using credit card, if the interest rate environment remains subdued.

- Age
  Age affects the spending level. Younger the population, higher the spending level.

e.g. India and African countries have median age below 30 years. While, European countries have median age of around 43 years. For US, it is 39 years.

- Level of Education
  More educated the population, higher the income level and hence more spending level is expected.

  e.g. As per 2011 census, only 4.5% of India's population is educated up to the level of graduation or above. As of 2019, 83.5 % of the EU population aged 20–24 had completed at least an upper secondary level of education (i.e. ISCED level 3 and above).

- Family size.

  Larger the family size, large the spending level.

Business Investment

It concerns with purchases made by business houses. If a purchase only replaces an existing item, then it doesn't add to GDP and isn't counted. Purchases must go towards creating new consumer goods to be counted into GDP.

These kinds of business investment expenditures include:

- Fixed Investments
  There are two different types of fixed investments by business houses – Residential and non-residential investment.

  Residential investments are towards residential constructions (single family home, condos, townhouses).

Non-Residential investments are towards commercial real estate or business equipment (such as, software, manufacturing equipment, capital goods, etc.).

- Change in private inventories

  A decrease in inventory orders usually means that businesses are seeing demand slowdown. As inventories build up, companies will cut back the production. If it continues for long period, then layoffs are imminent. So, the change in private inventories is an important leading indicator.

Government expenditures

Before understanding, Government revenue, we need to understand the sources of Government revenues.

Below is example of OECD Countries' sources of its tax revenue:

OECD Average Sources of Tax Revenue, 2014

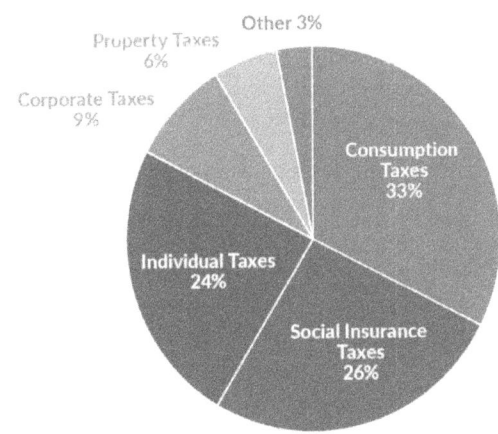

Source: OECD StatExtracts, http://stats.oecd.org

Government derives its revenue from below broader sources:

- Tax Revenue
  Personal Income tax, Wealth tax, GST/VAT, Corporate Tax, Excise
  Duty, custom Duty, Local Property Tax, Short/Long term Capital
  gain tax, Stamp Duty.

- Non-Tax Revenue
  Interest receipts (as received from loans given to states), railways
  revenue, Dividends and profits shares received from Government
  controlled public sector units. Dividends received from Central
  banks.

- Capital Revenue
  Revenue mopped up through disinvestment in Public sector units,
  domestic and foreign borrowings

- Grants

  Grants secured from various foreign agencies for economic and
  social cause.

Government's expenditures are broadly of two types:

- Current Expenditure
- Capital Expenditure

Current Expenditure

Money spent on a regular or ongoing basis. e.g. day to day provision of
essential services, operating costs and wages for public sector workers.
Those segments of expenditure are as below:

- Social protection
- Healthcare

- Education
- Justice
- Agriculture
- Defence
- Transport
- Tourism

Capital Expenditure

Money spent on "one-off" projects or on infrastructure that will have long-term benefits. Those segments of expenditure are as below:

- Public Transport (Building new rail networks, procuring new buses, engines, coaches).
- Health (building new hospital, buying new medical equipment, buying ambulances)
- Education (Building or extending schools, buying furniture, etc.)

e.g. below is the breakdown of Federal Government spending of India. States' share (23%), Interest Payment to service its debt (18%) and Federal program (12%) together has more than 50% share of total government spending.

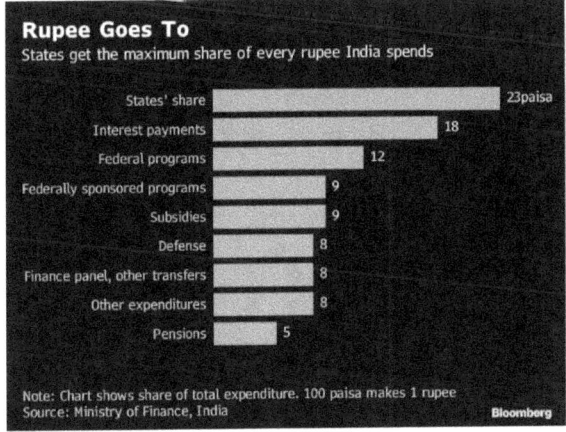

Rupee Goes To
States get the maximum share of every rupee India spends

States' share	23paisa
Interest payments	18
Federal programs	12
Federally sponsored programs	9
Subsidies	9
Defense	8
Finance panel, other transfers	8
Other expenditures	8
Pensions	5

Note: Chart shows share of total expenditure. 100 paisa makes 1 rupee
Source: Ministry of Finance, India

Bloomberg

Net Exports

"Net exports" is the fourth components of the GDP. There are variety of exported and imported goods and services, such as cars, consumer goods, films and software in a country. If a country exports $100 billion worth of goods and imports $75 billion worth of goods (exports > imports), then its net exported goods are $100 billion – $75 billion = $25 billion.

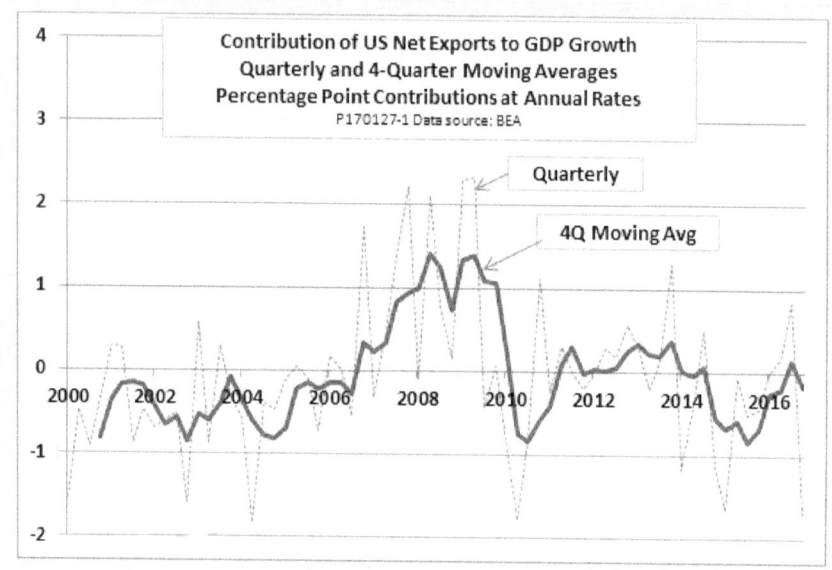

The above chart shows the contribution of "Net Exports" to US overall GDP from 2000-2016. This contribution has varied over these periods.

Analysis of Major countries and its GDP

We will analyse the GDP Growth rate of major countries over years and their GDP's contributing factor. We will try to understand which contributing factor has been more significant.

UNITED STATES

Below chart of US Historical GDP Growth rate, reveals that the contribution of "personal consumption" into overall GDP varied across the past 7 decades.

Average annual GDP Growth rate has seen a constant drop from 8% level during 1950's. It fell down to average rate of 6% during 1960's.

From 1970's to 2000's, average rate fell to 4% level. From 2000's to 2019, average rate fell to 2-3% level.

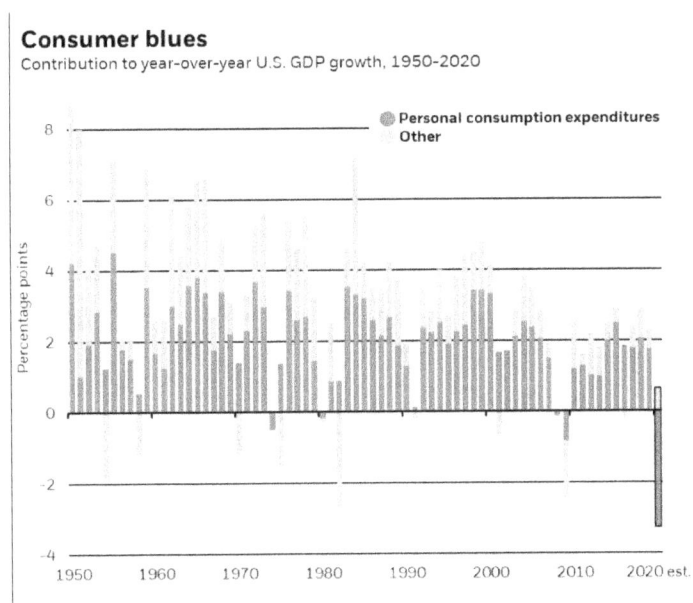

Consumer blues
Contribution to year-over-year U.S. GDP growth, 1950-2020

Source: Blackrock

As GDP growth rate slowed down over the year, contribution of "personal consumption" on GDP increased and contribution of "other" factor decreased. It reflects the changing dynamics of US economy.

Bad GDP Years for UNITED STATES

Some years proved to be quite a bad year for the GDP growth such as, 1982, 2009 and 2020 (estimated). In all these 3 years real GDP growth rate contracted by more than 1%.

Year 1982

- GDP Decline: -1.8%
- Peak unemployment rate: 10.8%

Reasons/causes:

Between 1980-82 the US economy experienced a deep recession; the primary reason was the disinflationary monetary policy adopted by the Federal Reserve. Inflation had reached 13.5%.

The Federal Reserve raised interest rates and slowed money supply growth. It slowed the economy and caused unemployment to rise. Energy prices and supply were put at risk causing a confidence crisis as well as inflation. This long and deep recession was caused by the regime change in Iran. The world's second-largest producer of oil at the time, the country overthrew it's US backed government.

Year 2009

- GDP Decline: -2.5%
- Peak unemployment rate: 10%

Reasons/causes:

The housing price bubble of 2000's burst ultimately and resulted in a record foreclosure. This turned into a systemic risk and a financial crisis that threw the markets worldwide into a tailspin. Oil prices spiked to record highs by mid-2008 and then crashed, devastating the US oil industry.

Year 2020

- GDP Decline: -5.9% (IMF estimates)
- Peak unemployment rate: Estimated to be 16% (in April 2020 from 4.4% in March 2020).

Reasons/causes:

In January 2020, world witnessed a severe Pandemic COVID-19 originated from China. It was perceived to be extremely contagious (at the level of 1918 Spanish Flu pandemic; much more than 1957 Asian Flu and 1968 Hong Kong Flu Pandemic).

This resulted in strict containment measures imposed across the world. It impacted both demand and supply side of the economy. There is no vaccine for this Pandemic yet, so economic impact of this Pandemic could get worsened as time passes.

CHINA

China GDP Growth contributors – Personal consumptions, Business investment, Government expenditures and net exports – have varied across the past 2 decades.

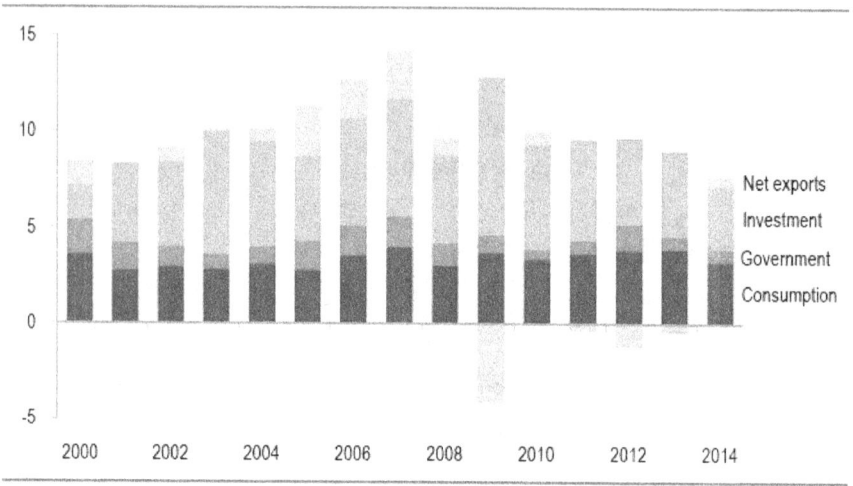

Chart 2: Contributions to real GDP growth
Ppt, 2011-14 forecasts

Sources: CEIC, Standard Chartered Research

Government expenditure has contributed to overall GDP growth rate around 1-2% point over 15 years periods in above chart. It translates into 10-15% contribution.

Personal consumption has contributed to overall GDP growth rate around 3-4% point over 15 years periods in above chart. It translates into 30-45% contribution.

Private investment has contributed to overall GDP growth rate around 2-9% point over 15 years periods in above chart. It translates into 25-80% contribution.

Net Exports has contributed to overall GDP growth rate around -4 to 3% point over 15 years periods in above chart. It translates into minus 50% to 30% contribution.

On an overall level, GDP Growth rate from 2000-08, growth rate has been at an average rate of whopping 10% level. It got slowed down to 8% level after global financial crisis of 2008. Since last 2 years (2018-2019), it has further fallen to 6-6.5% level. In 2020, its economy is expected to grow by a meagre rate of 1.2% (as per IMF estimates) because of adverse impact of 2020 COVID-19 Pandemic.

Bad GDP Years for CHINA

China has witnessed quite encouraging GDP growth rate since 1980. But year 1989 and 1990 has been quite dismal year for china's economy. It registered a GDP growth of 4.2% in 1989 and 3.9% in 1990.

Reasons/causes:

China's GDP growth slowed drastically in the aftermath of the Tiananmen massacre that happened in June 1989. Several countries, including the US, imposed trade sanctions against China, and Chinese economic reforms were essentially put on hold.

China's real GDP growth rate fell from an impressive 11.3% in 1988 to a dismal 4.2% in 1989. GDP growth rate declined further to 3.9% in 1990. In 1991, economic reforms were restarted and foreign sanctions against China were reduced, and real GDP grew by 9.2%.

GERMANY

Below are two charts of Germany historical GDP growth rate and contribution of personal consumption (as % of total GDP) since 1970. GDP Growth Rate ranged between -6% to 5% from 1970-2018.

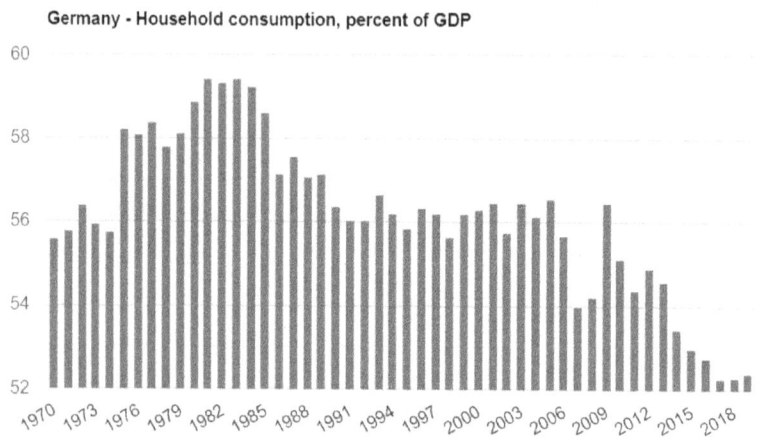

Germany - Household consumption, percent of GDP

Source: Global economy.com

Contribution of "personal consumption" to GDP has been consistently declining from 59% in 1970 to 52% in 2018.

It shows that economy's dependence on "personal consumption" has reduced over the year. You may see in below bar-chart that economy's dependence on "Net exports" increased during the same period.

Net exports contribution to GDP was 15.1% in 1970. This contribution increased to 46.9% in 2018.

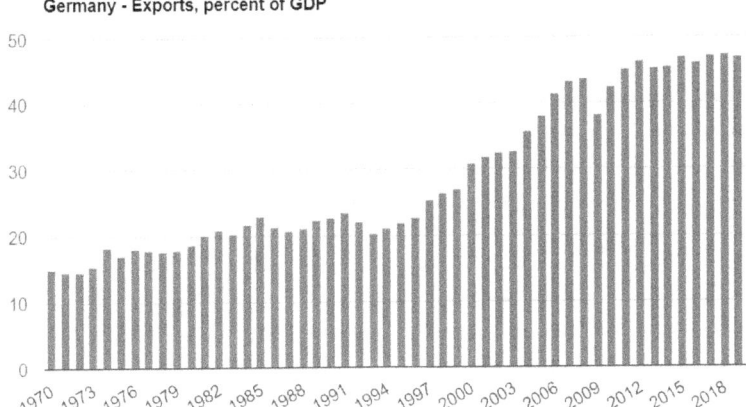

Germany - Exports, percent of GDP

Source: Global economy.com

Bad GDP Years for GERMANY

During the last 4 decades, Germany has witnessed 4 contractions (i.e. negative GDP growth years) – 1982, 1993, 2003 and 2009.

In 1982, GDP growth rate contracted to -0.8%. It was structural issue for German economy. Schmidt's coalition government collapsed in late 1982. The new government proceeded to implement new policies to reduce the government role in the economy. The state role in the West German economy declined from 52% to 46% of GDP between 1982 and 1990, according to Bundesbank (German central bank) statistics.

In 1993, GDP growth rate went down to -1% level. Germany struggled to overcome the twin effects of - global slowdown (of early 90s) and the task of rebuilding the former communist east Germany.

In 2003, GDP growth rate went down to -0.7% level and in 2009, GDP growth rate went down to -5.6% level because global financial crisis (subprime meltdown).

INDIA

During the past two decades, India's growth rate has been at 7-8% level. Contribution of Private consumption has been quite significant consistently at average level of 4% point to overall GDP growth rate.

Contribution of Business investment has varied across these 2 decades period. It varied from 1-7% (average 3%) point contribution to overall GDP growth rate. Private Investment is second largest contributors to GDP growth. Contribution of "Government spending" and "Net exports" to GDP growth are quite inconsistent.

"Net exports" has not contributed consistently to overall GDP. In most of the years (between 2010-18), Net exports had a negative contribution to GDP (i.e. imports were higher than exports).

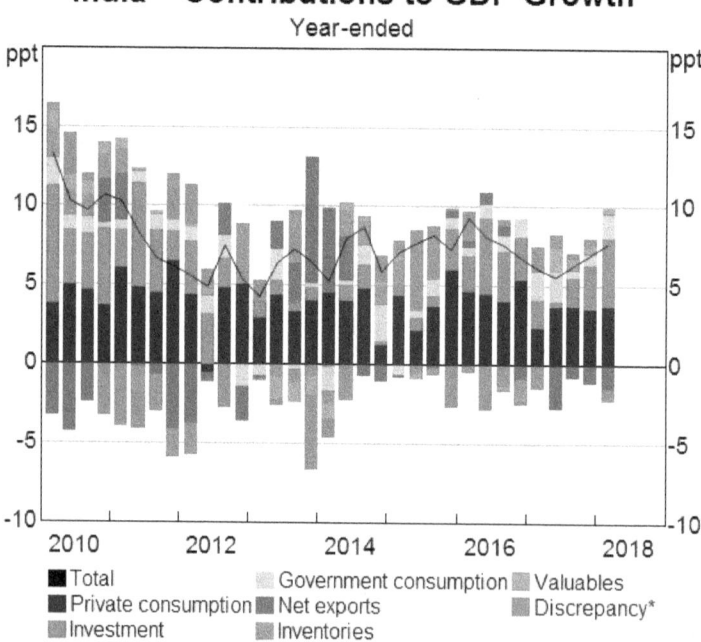

India – Contributions to GDP Growth
Year-ended

*   Equal to difference between total GDP and the sum of its components
Sources: CEIC Data: RBA

Bad GDP Years for INDIA

Since 1965 till now, India has witnessed a decent GDP growth though below-par the growth registered in China. India had its share of bad GDP growth rate year as well, particularly in 1965-66, 1966-67, 1972-73, 1979-80, 1991-92 and 2020-21.

India had started large scale economic reform from 1991 onwards. All the economic contractions or drastic drop in GDP prior to 1990s, were attributed to the severe droughts or high international energy prices. Prior to 1990, the farm sector accounted for the dominant share of GDP, and given weak external balances, economy was quite vulnerable to energy or commodity prices.

Below are bad economic years for India and its GDP growth rate

1957-58: (-1.2%)
1965-66: (-2.6%)
1966-67: (-0.1%)
1972-73: (-0.6%)
1979-80: (-5.2%)
1991-92: (1.43%)

In 1979-80, the Indian economy witnessed a twin adverse effect of a severe drought in the country and a spike in crude oil prices (it almost doubled due to supply disruptions owing to the Iranian revolution). Because of the drought, the agricultural production declined by a sharp 10%. The sharp rise in crude oil prices attributed to sudden rise in inflationary pressure with wholesale price inflation soaring to an astronomical level of 20%.

The year 1979-80 was a politically unstable year for India. It witnessed change in the government, with the fall of the 33-month old coalition government under the Janata Party. In 1980, Indira Gandhi came back to power after emergency with a massive mandate.

India's economic woes started worsening since 1985 as the imports increased. By the end of 1990, in the run-up to the Gulf War, India was in such a dire economic situation that its foreign exchange reserves could have barely financed three weeks' worth of imports. By July 1990, the low reserves had led to a sharp depreciation of the rupee, which in turn exacerbated the twin deficit problem.

The Chandrasekhar government could not pass the budget in February 1991 after Moody downgraded India's bond ratings. The ratings further deteriorated, because of which India could not seek short term loans. The World Bank and IMF also withdrew their economic assistance, leaving the government with no option except to mortgage the country's gold to avoid defaulting on payments.

Chapter-3

Business Cycles – How it affects the GDP and Markets

- How business cycle affects the GDP
- Business Cycles – Its impact on Markets
  - ➢ Equity/Stock Markets
  - ➢ Bond Markets

How business cycle affects the GDP

Business cycle defines how a country's real GDP growth fluctuates over time. It goes through different phases in a succession, as aggregate output increases and decreases over a period. Over a long-run, the business cycle shows a steady increase in the potential output in a growing economy.

There are five different stages in the business cycle (in the mentioned order) - expansion, peak, recession or contraction, depression, trough, and recovery.

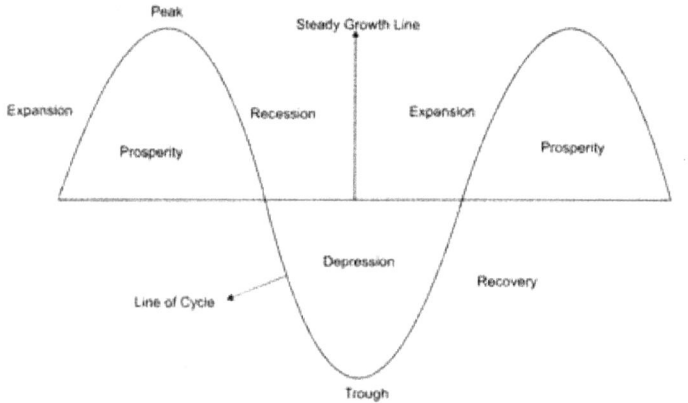

Figure-2: Representation of Phases of a Business Cycle

Although depression stage is a rare stage and not always reached on the way down in a full business cycle.

EXPANSION

The stage of cycle that moves above the steady growth line represents the expansion phase of a business cycle. In this phase, there is an increase in various factors, such as production, employment, output, wages, profits, demand and supply of products, and sales.

In this stage, the prices of factor of production and output increases simultaneously. In this phase, borrowers are capable of repaying their debts; therefore, interest rates are higher. This leads to an increase in the flow of money.

During expansion stage, due to increase in investment opportunities, Industry operates at its maximum utilization level.

PEAK

The momentum of expansion stage eventually slows down and tops out. This stage is known as peak stage. During peak stage, the factors, such as production, profit, sales, and employment, are higher, but it reaches it saturation level. There is a gradual decrease in the demand of various products due to increase in the prices of input.

The increase in the prices of input leads to an increase in the prices of final products, though income or wage of an individual remains unchanged. As a result, the demand for discretionary products, such as jewellery, homes, automobiles, refrigerators and other durables, starts falling.

RECESSION

As noticed during the peak stage, there is a gradual decrease in the demand of various products due to increase in the prices of input. When the decline in the demand of products becomes rapid and steady, the recession phase takes place.

In recession stage, all the factors, such as production, prices, saving and investment, starts decreasing. Because of the lagging economic data does not capture the prevailing ground-reality, the Producers are usually unaware of such decrease in the demand of products and they end up continuing to produce goods and services. This results in, supply of products exceeds the demand.

As time passes producers realize the surplus level of supply when the cost of manufacturing of a product is more than profit generated. This condition soon spreads to all industries.

As the problem exists for a longer duration, producers start noticing it. Consequently, producers avoid any type of further investment in factor of production. This leads to the reduction in the prices of factor, which results in the decline of demand of inputs as well as output.

TROUGH

During this stage, the economic activities of a country decline below its historical average level. In this phase, the growth rate of an economy becomes negative. In addition, there is a rapid decline in government tax receipts and government expenditures.

In this phase, it becomes difficult for the leveraged corporate houses to pay off their debts. As a result, the rate of interest decreases; therefore, banks credit growth declines. Consequently, banks face the situation of increase in their cash balances.

GDP growth of a country drops significantly, and unemployment rate becomes higher. Investors feel the brunt of stock markets crash. Many weak firms are forced to leave industries or get dissolved. The economy reaches to the lowest level of shrinking.

RECOVERY

As noticed during trough stage that economy reaches to the lowest level of shrinking. This lowest level is the limit to which an economy shrinks. Once the economy touches this lowest level, a new journey of economic recovery begins.

Individuals and organizations start developing a positive attitude toward the various economic factors, such as investment, employment, and production. This process of reversal starts from the labour market. Firms starts hiring in a limited number. Wages provided to individuals is less as compared to their skills and abilities. This marks the beginning of the recovery stage.

Consumers increase their rate of consumption, as they assume that there would be no further reduction in the prices of products. As a result, the demand for consumer products increases.

Banks start utilizing their accumulated cash balances by declining the lending rate and increasing investment in various securities and bonds. Private investors start investing in the stock market. security prices increase and rate of interest decreases.

How long does each economic business cycle last?

Below is one such example for US economy from March 1991 to November 2001. This full business cycle, from Recovery to peak, took almost 10 years and peak to contraction took just 6 months.

Figure 1

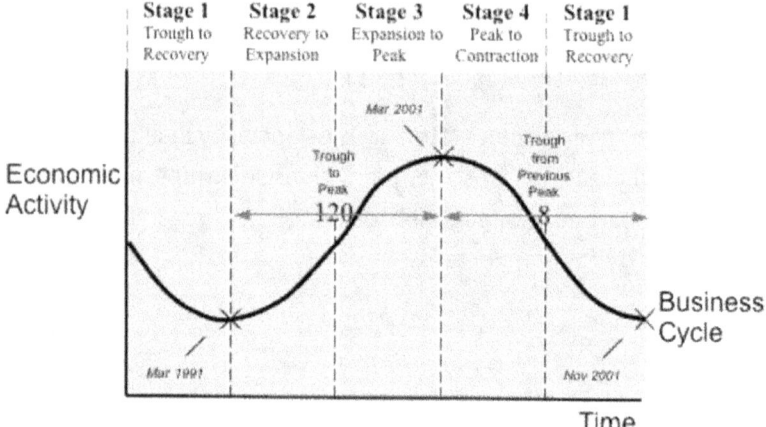

One of the important phases of business cycle is "Recession". Each recession is different and how long would it linger on, depends on the policy-response to it. Let's take a look at all the historical recession period in US (since 1950) and how long did it last:

U.S. recession since 1950	
Period	Duration, months
1953-54	10
1957-58	8
1960-61	10
1969-70	11
1973-75	16
1980	6
1981-82	16
1990-91	8
2001	8
2007-09	18

In all the previous 10 recessionary periods, the recession lasted for 6-18 months. This provides a guideline for our future recessionary periods.

Business Cycles – Its impact on Markets

It is obvious that all Markets (Equity, Bond or FX) always expect a healthy GDP growth number for a country. But as we saw in previous chapters that there are various stages of business cycle in any country. So, it is very important to understand, in which business cycle a country's economy is in. Depending on that prevailing stage of business cycle, stock markets or bond markets or FX markets perform.

Stock Markets

From March 1991 to March 2001, as per the business cycle, the US economy was undergoing "recovery -> Expansion" stage. This stage is usually the best phase for stock market's return.

We can see in below chart that the S&P 500 (US Benchmark Index) had performed so well during this period. The index level had tripled during this period. A persistent level of good stock market performance is loosely called "Bullish" markets by investment fraternity.

S&P500 peaked in mid-2000, just few months before the business cycle was officially considered to be at peak level (in March 2001).

A sharp fall of S&P500 Index (of almost 75%) was observed during Peak -> Contraction -> Recovery phase (from mid-2000 to 2002).

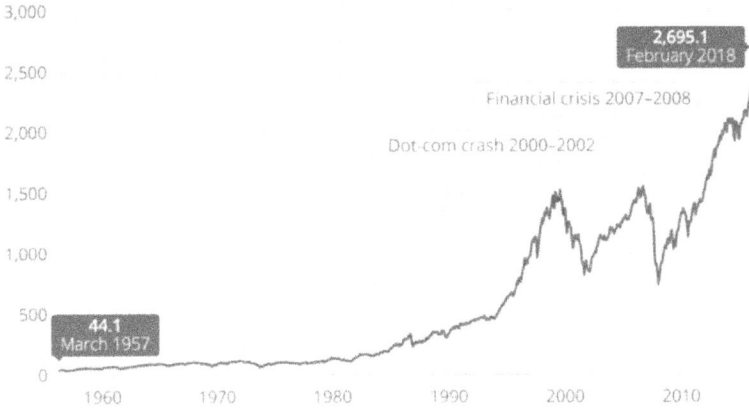

During Early cycle, companies belonging to Real estate, consumer discretionary and Industrials sectors are expected to do exceptionally well. Financials, Information Technology and Materials sector are expected to do fairly well.

During Mid cycle, communication services sector is expected to do fairly well.

During Late cycle, Materials, Consumer Staples, Health Care, Energy sectors are expected to exceptionally well. While Utilities sector are expected to do fairly well.

	Early cycle Rebounds	Mid cycle Peaks	Late cycle Moderates	Recession cycle Contracts
Financials	+			
Real Estate	++			--
Consumer Discretionary	++	--	--	
Information Technology	+	+	--	--
Industrials	++			--
Materials	+	--	++	
Consumer Staples			++	++
Health Care	--		++	++
Energy	--		++	
Communication Services		+		-
Utilities	--	-	+	++
	Economically sensitive sectors may tend to outperform, while more defensive sectors have tended to underperform.	Making marginal portfolio allocation changes to manage drawdown risk with sectors may enhance risk-adjusted returns during this cycle.	Defensive and inflation-resistant sectors tend to perform better, while more cyclical sectors underperform.	Since performance is generally negative in recessions, investors should focus on the most defensive, historically stable sectors.

During Recession cycle, Consumer Staples, Health Care and Utilities sectors are expected to do exceptionally well.

Bonds Markets

Bond markets usually follows the inflation rate level. Inflation rate remains subdued during "Recovery to Expansion" phase of business cycle.

As per the below inflation rate graph, inflation rate got bottomed out in 1998, somewhere close to beginning of expansion phase of business cycle. This was the time (as per below US 10 Year benchmark Yield), when the Bond's yield had also hit its bottom level (Yield close to 4.5% level).

Inflation rate started increasing after 1998 till 2000. In 2000, it peaked out. As per the business cycle, this was the time, just a few months before the peak stage of the business cycle. During the same time, as per below US 10 Year benchmark Yield, the Bond yield also topped out (Yield close to 6.5% level).

United States: Inflation rate

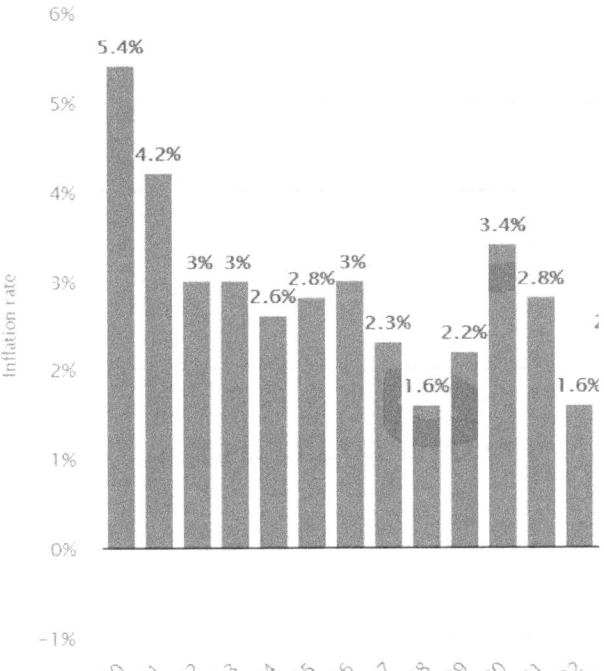

United States 10 Year Bond Yield (1991-2008)-

Bad loans (NPAs) Over a full Business Cycle

Credit cycle in the economy gets affected by prevailing business cycle.
Recovery-to-peak phase usually is the best phase for bank's credit
business. In the below example for Indian economy, we can see that the
Non-performing loans (NPAs or bad loans) reduces from its peak level
during Recovery-to-peak phase of the business cycle.

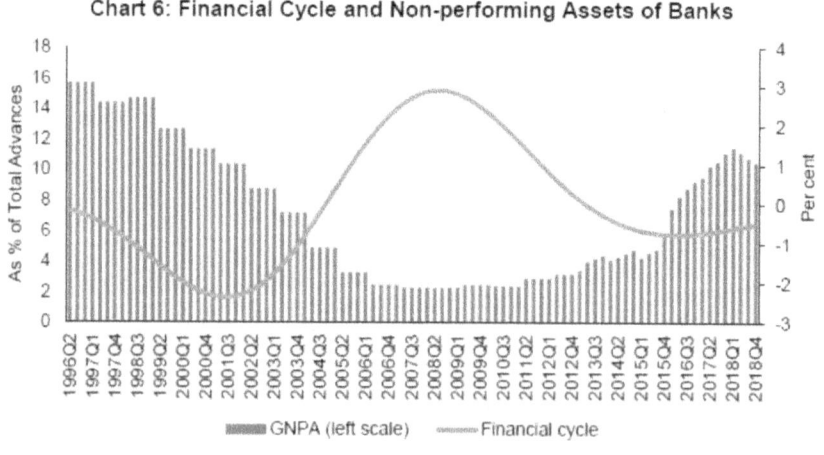

Chart 6: Financial Cycle and Non-performing Assets of Banks

Source: RBI

Chapter-4

GDP growth – Key Input factors & its % contribution

- Overview
- Asian economies
- Rest of the world

Overview

There are three key input factors that drive economic growth:

- Accumulation of capital stock through investment
- Increase in labour inputs, such as workers or number of hours worked
- Technological advancement, also known "total factor productivity (TFP)".

A country's growth can be analysed further by understanding what percentage of economic growth comes from three important factors – capital input, labour input and technological advancement.

Over the last few decades, in most economies across the world, we have witnessed a tremendous growth in economic activities. This growth has been driven primarily by factor accumulation. i.e. by increases in the "size of the labour force" and by increases in the "capital stock" through investment.

At the same time, significant increases in productivity, particularly in labour productivity, have also taken place across the world. Strengthening productivity is a critical element for the sustained and more resilient growth.

While a large pool of surplus labour has been absorbed in many economies, so the factor "Labour input" (i.e. new bunch of labour pool getting added to economy every year) may not be significant for such economies. In order to compensate for this, such economies have focused on "Productivity growth".

It has been observed that "Productivity growth" is significant for the economies where the size of the labour force is forecast to stagnate due to low population growth and less young population.

Moreover, it is very imperative for such countries to pass on the productivity gains to labour force and strengthen its investment in human resources to further improve productivity and competitiveness. This is also important from the perspective of addressing inequalities in the low-to-medium income economies.

A country, having a higher "level" of productivity, is able to produce more with the same amount of labour inputs and is thus comparatively more competitive. This results in countries, having higher productivity "growth", experience a larger relative increase in their output (i.e. GDP) than those with lower productivity "growth" rates.

Across sectors, productivity of industrial and manufacturing sector tends to grow faster than the productivity of agricultural sector because of adaptability for technological change and economies of scale.

As the share of the manufacturing sector in GDP increases, so does the productivity growth, as labour moves from a relatively low productivity sector (e.g. agriculture) to a higher productivity sector (e.g. manufacturing).

Though, these factor accumulation (contribution of labour force Vs capital stock) has varied from country to country. It has also been affected by different stages of Business cycle within a country.

Asian Economies

The Percentage contribution of input factors (Physical capital & Labour force) and total factor productivity to output growth for Asian economies:

Countries	1990s			2000s			1990-2011		
	Physical capital	Labour force	TFP	Physical capital	Labour force	TFP	Physical capital	Labour force	TFP
Armenia	-2.7	-34.6	137.3	25.8	0.2	73.9	13.6	-14.7	101.1
Australia	49.4	-18.4	68.9	64.5	56.7	-21.2	58.0	24.6	17.4
China	45.0	8.2	46.7	63.4	4.6	32.0	55.6	6.1	38.3
Fiji	9.4	34.4	56.2	14.4	13.7	72.0	11.9	24.0	64.1
India	59.1	14.0	27.0	48.5	16.2	35.3	53.0	15.2	31.8
Indonesia	82.9	17.0	0.1	57.5	15.2	27.4	68.3	15.9	15.7
Iran (Islamic Republic of)	21.4	30.3	48.3	55.9	30.3	13.8	38.7	30.3	31.0
Japan	75.8	20.5	3.7	14.3	5.8	79.9	45.0	13.1	41.8
Kazakhstan	-23.4	-15.6	138.9	42.1	14.4	43.5	14.0	1.5	84.4
Kyrgyzstan	-4.1	17.9	86.2	21.3	21.8	56.9	8.6	19.8	71.6
Malaysia	48.3	19.5	32.2	50.8	22.0	27.2	49.7	21.0	29.3
Mongolia	15.4	1.4	83.3	23.3	21.4	55.3	19.9	12.8	67.3
New Zealand	37.5	32.2	30.3	64.9	35.0	0.1	51.2	33.6	15.2
Philippines	30.4	38.2	31.4	68.1	27.8	4.1	52.0	32.3	15.8
Republic of Korea	50.9	20.8	28.3	60.1	19.6	20.3	55.5	20.2	24.3
Russian Federation	-2.0	3.2	98.8	4.7	7.6	87.7	1.3	5.4	93.3
Singapore	59.3	21.2	19.4	40.1	9.9	50.0	49.7	15.6	34.7
Sri Lanka	21.4	25.6	53.0	22.2	28.8	48.9	21.9	27.4	50.7
Tajikistan	-12.3	3.6	108.7	-16.3	2.9	113.4	-14.6	3.2	111.4
Thailand	45.2	3.0	51.7	38.5	24.4	37.1	41.9	13.7	44.4
Turkey	75.8	17.5	6.7	69.7	13.2	17.0	72.3	15.1	12.6

Sources: ESCAP calculations, based on Penn world table 8.1. See Robert C. Feenstra, Robert Inklaar and Marcel P. Timmer. "The next generation of the Penn world table", American Economic Review, vol. 105, No. 10, pp. 3150-3182.

Contribution of "Labour force" factor in the output growth

Below bar-chart gives us details about the labour force contribution in the output growth across two broader time periods – 1990s and 2000s.

India, New Zealand and Australia witnessed an increase in labour force contribution over these 2 decades. It might have happened for 3 reasons – a) New workforce got added to economy or b) labour force productivity has increased over these periods or c) relative contribution of "physical capital" & TFP together have fallen.

While, China, Singapore and Japan saw a decline in labour force contribution to output growth.

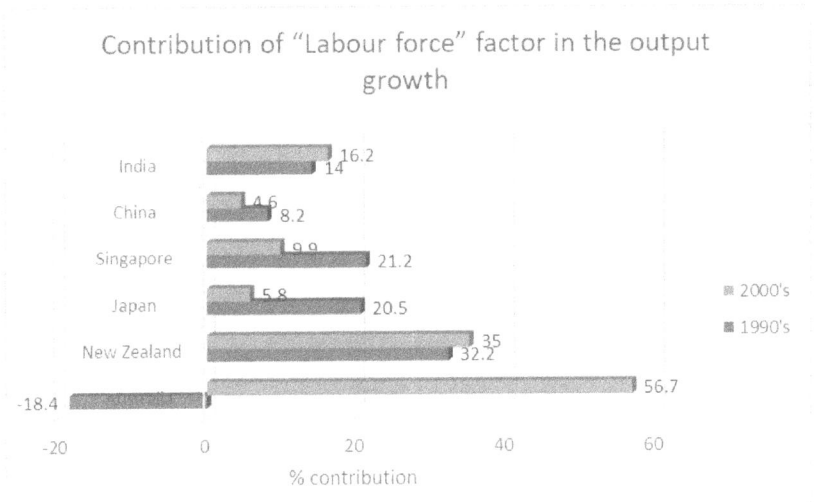

Contribution of "Labour force" factor in the output growth

% contribution

- 2000's
- 1990's

India: 16.2 / 14
China: 4.6 / 8.2
Singapore: 9.9 / 21.2
Japan: 5.8 / 20.5
New Zealand: 35 / 32.2
56.7
-18.4

Contribution of "Physical Capital" factor in the output growth

Below bar-chart tells us about the physical capital contribution in the output growth across two broader time periods – 1990s and 2000s.

China, New Zealand and Australia witnessed an increase in physical capital contribution over these 2 decades. It might have happened for 3 reasons – a) New capital got added to economy or b) capital productivity has increased over these periods or c) relative contribution of "labour force" & TFP together have fallen.

While, India, Singapore and Japan saw a decline in Physical capital contribution to output growth.

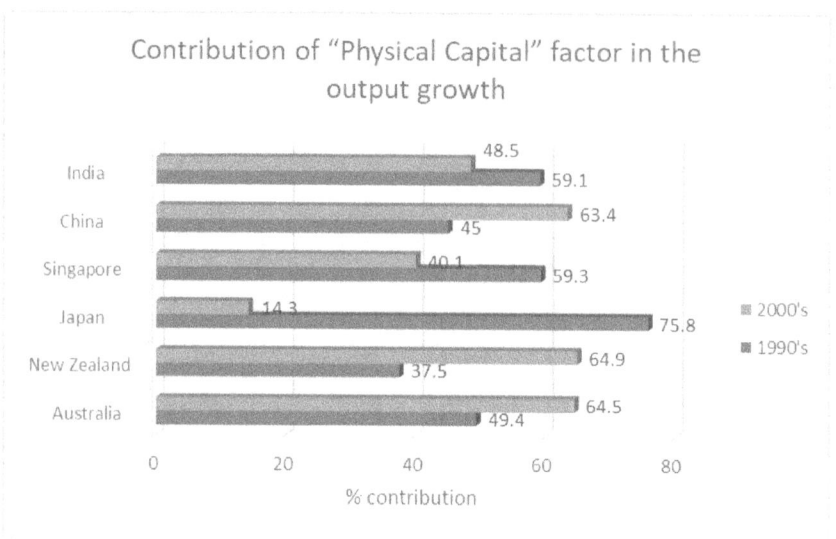

Contribution of "Physical Capital" factor in the output growth

Country	2000's	1990's
India	48.5	59.1
China	63.4	45
Singapore	40.1	59.3
Japan	14.3	75.8
New Zealand	64.9	37.5
Australia	64.5	49.4

% contribution

Contribution of "Total factor Productivity" factor in the output growth

Below bar-chart tells us about total factor productivity (TFP) contribution in the output growth across 2 broader time periods – 1990s and 2000s.

India, Singapore and Japan witnessed an increase in TFP contribution over these 2 decades. It might have happened because of technical advancement during this period.

While, China, New Zealand and Australia saw a decline in TFP contribution to output growth.

Contribution of Total factor Productivity (TFP) in the output growth

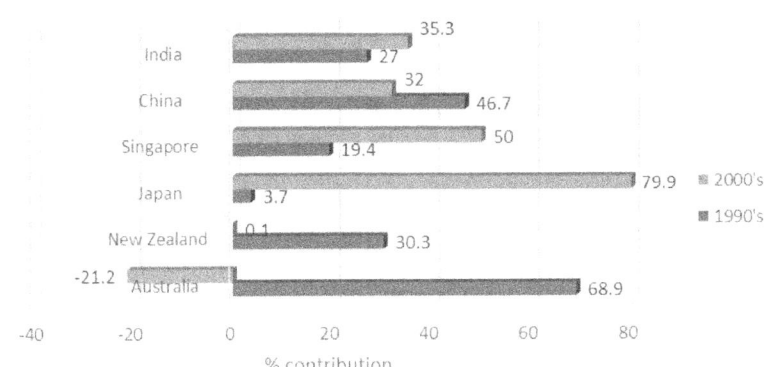

Chapter-5

GDP Growth – Key Driving forces and determinants of higher Growth

- Key Driving forces of economic growth
  - ➢ High Income countries (Higher GDP per capita)
  - ➢ Medium Income Countries (Medium GDP per capita)
  - ➢ Low Income Countries (lower GDP per capita)

Driving forces of Economic Growth

We have always wondered why some countries have witnessed an accelerated economic development while other major economies have lagged. What economic policies, technological development and efficient institutions have ensured such economic development in few selected economies?

We will perhaps not be able to analyse all countries in this book. But we can analyse these countries by clubbing all these countries into 3 distinct groups –

1. High Income countries i.e. High GDP per capita economies – e.g. OECD Countries (a group of more than 36 countries)
2. Medium Income countries i.e. Medium GDP per capita economies – e.g. BRICs
3. Low Income countries i.e. Low GDP per capita economies – e.g. Central African countries.

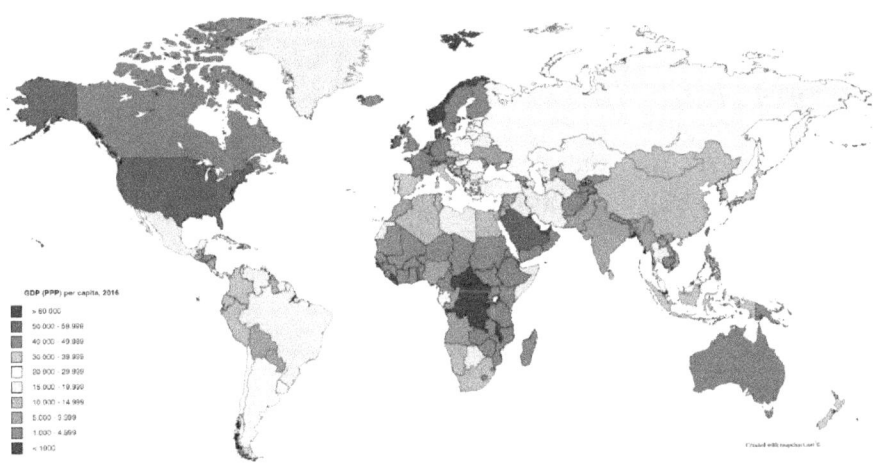

The economic efficiency in many countries has been achieved by the help of varied factors – Accumulation of physical capital, human capital, research and development activity, macroeconomic/Structural policy settings, trade policy and financial market conditions.

Determinants of economic growth

The deciding economic or political factors that affect the country's economic growth are-

- Externalities
- Accumulation of physical capital
- Human Capital
- Research & Development
- Monetary Policy
- Inflation
- Fiscal Policy
- Financial Development
- Financial depth
  - Broad money (M2/GDP)
- Private Investment
- International Trade
- Remittances Inflow

Externalities

Externalities such as Political uncertainties & Policy change usually affect GDP growth only in the short to medium-term by shifting the growth path, although the underlying rate of growth are driven by population growth and technical progress (Usually, varies across countries).

Accumulation of physical capital

The rate of accumulation of physical capital is one of the main factors determining the level of GDP per capita. It impacts the economy permanently provided the technological innovation is embedded into new capital.

How the capital accumulation is utilized by the economy to convert it into growth term, this is also very significant. It varies across countries and differs in the investment rate. Hence the GDP per capita also differs across these countries. Investment rate measurement is done for Private Sector as well as for Public Sector. The long-run averages of Private-sector investment rates range from around 10-20% of GDP.

Human Capital

Basic skills and experience of labour force, belonging to a nation, represent a form of capital (which is termed as "Human Capital"). Investment in human capital (e.g. expenditures on education & training) usually has a permanent impact on the long-term growth provided research & development and adoption of new technologies is facilitated by a highly skilled workforce.

The average number of years of formal education among the working-age population usually represents the human capital of a nation. When it comes to the level of educational attainment, there are significant differences across the countries. In 1970, across OECD countries, the average length of formal education of the working age population ranged between 5.7 years (Spain) to 11.6 years (United States).

For OECD economies, it took almost 2 decades to change this range to 7.7 years to 13.6 years (Portugal and Germany, respectively). Spain (From 5.7 years to 8.8 years) is no longer at the lowest range; it leapfrogged Portugal (From 6.6 years to 7.7 years) in a period of 2 decades. While the US (From 11.6 years to 12.8 years) is no longer at the highest range; Germany (From 9.8 years to 13.6 years) leapfrogged the US in a period of 2 decades.

It indicates that the increase in average length of education ranges from less than half a year on average per decade (e.g. the United States) to more than one year on average per decade (e.g. Germany and Italy, the latter from a relatively low level).

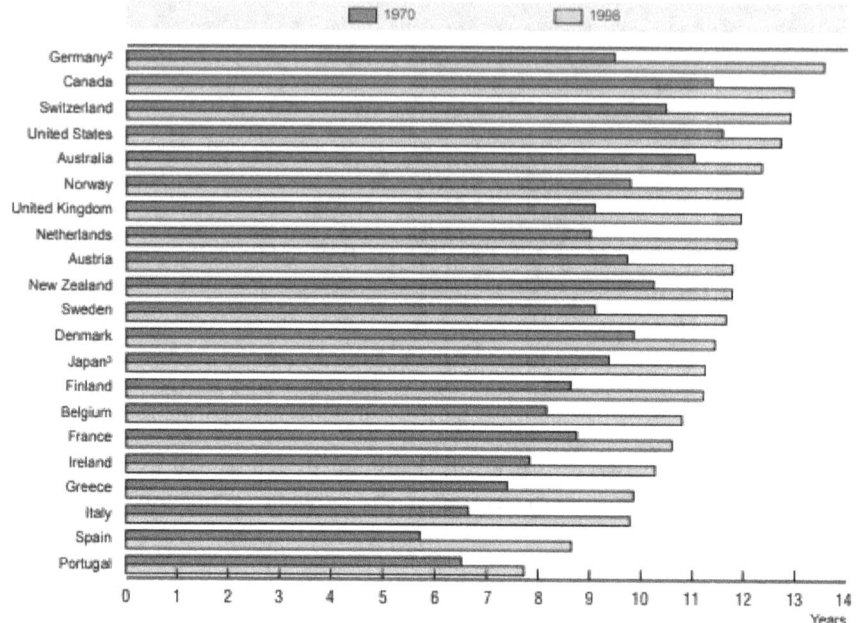

Figure 2. **Average years of education[1] of the working-age population in OECD countries**
1970 and 1998

1. Average number of years of education in the population aged 15-64 years, based on data on level of education attained and assumptions about the number of years of education implied by different levels of education attainment.
2. Western Germany in 1970.
3. 1990 instead of 1998 for Japan.
Source: OECD.

Research & Development

Expenditure on research and development (R&D) is investment in knowledge. This further translates into new technologies and more efficient ways of using physical and human capital.

There seems to be stronger consensus that R&D usually has a persistent effect on growth i.e. higher R&D expenditure would be associated with permanently higher growth rates. Government policy needs to facilitate the private-sector investment in R&D through direct and indirect measures. Direct measures include provision or funding. Indirect measures include tax incentives and protection of intellectual property rights to encourage private-sector R&D.

Role of R&D on growth needs to be assessed very delicately. Public sector R&D expenditure (usually in defence or medicinal research) often does not contribute to growth immediately or it takes a while to contribute to growth. So, we must differentiate between various type of R&D expenditure.

In OECD Countries, Overall expenditure on R&D as % of GDP has risen since the 1980s in most OECD countries. Below bar-chart reveals the additional details about R&D expenses in OECD countries and changes in expenses over a decade time.

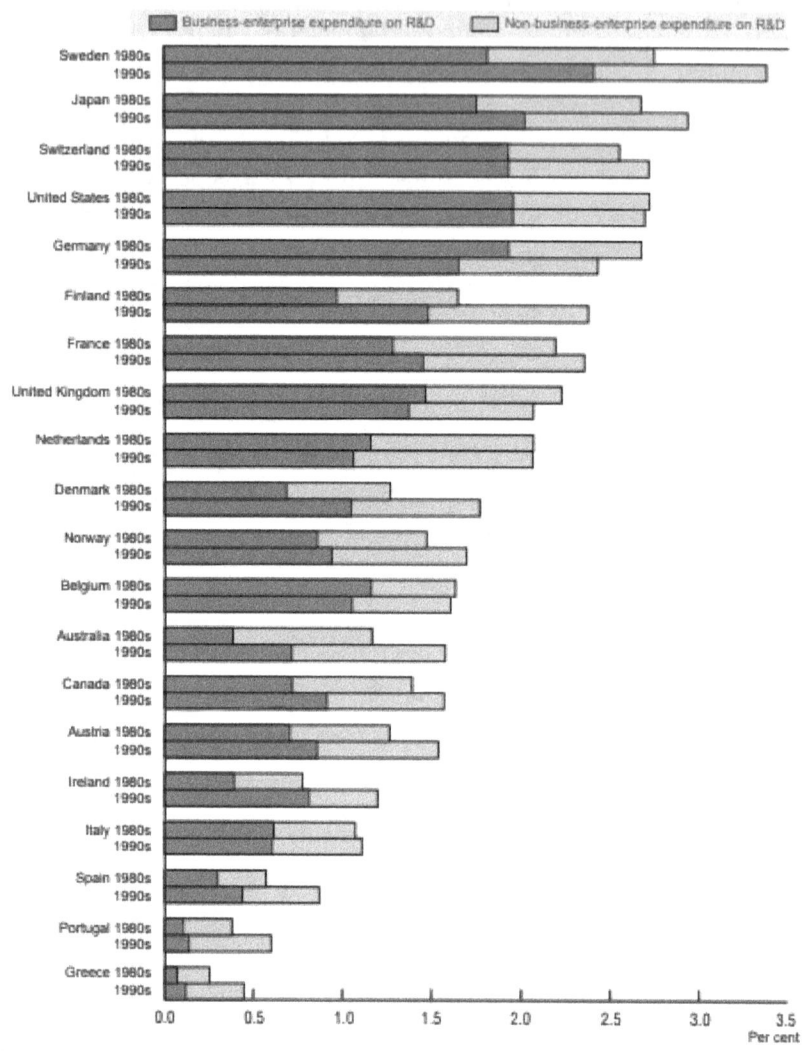

Figure 3. **Expenditure on R&D in the OECD countries**

1980s and 1990s

Total expenditure on R&D as a percentage of GDP

Monetary Policy

Monetary policy is action that a country's central bank can take to influence how much money is in the economy and how much does it cost to borrow. Monetary policy decision affects how much prices are increasing (which is known as inflation rate). Low and stable inflation is good for the economy.

A better monetary policy is the backbone of a healthy and prosperous economy. All the global economies have a separate body named "Central Bank" or "Monetary Agency" to carry out such Macroeconomic or monetary policies. In US, it is called "Federal Reserve Bank" (FED). In Europe, it is ECB. In UK, it is Bank of England. India, it is RBI.

Only a politically independent Central bank can ensure a sustainable monetary policy. Different Monetary agencies have different set of objectives in conducting monetary policy:

Country	Monetary Agency	Monetary Policy		Past 10 Year GDP Growth rate
		Objective-1	Objective-2	
US	FED	Maximum Employment (to keep longer run normal unemployment rate between 3.5-4.5%)	Stable prices (Keep Inflation rate close to 2% as measured by PCE)	Close to 2%
EUROZONE	ECB	Stable prices (Keep Inflation rate under control as measured by HICP)	n/a	Close to 1%
Japan	BOJ	Stable prices (Keep Inflation rate close to 2% as measured by CPI)	n/a	Close to 1.5%
UK	BOE	Stable prices (Keep Inflation rate close to 2%)	n/a	Close to 1.5%
Canada	BOC	Stable prices (Keep Inflation rate close to 2% as measured by CPI)	Flexible Exchange Rate	Close to 2%
Australia	RBA	Stable prices (Keep Inflation rate between 2-3% as measured by CPI)	n/a	Close to 2.5%
China	PBOC	Stable Exchange Rate	n/a	Close to 8%
India	RBI	Stable prices (Keep Inflation rate between 2-6% as measured by CPI)	n/a	Close to 7%

Inflation

Price stability is a necessary precondition to sustainable growth for any economies. Globally, it is usually track monthly through Consumer Price Index (CPI). CPI is primarily a measure of goods and services targeted towards individuals and consumed by individuals. It is represented in % terms and computed as % change in the current month CPI Index Vs similar figure a year ago, same month.

Inflation rate is usually manoeuvred by monetary agency using the policy rate based on an assessment of the current and evolving macroeconomic situation; and modulation of liquidity conditions to anchor money market rates at or around the policy rate. Policy rate changes transmit through the money market to the entire the financial system, which, in turn, influences aggregate demand – a key determinant of inflation and growth.

Country	Name of Index	CPI Components (% Weightage in overall CPI)									
		Food & beverages	Housing	Apparel	Medical care	Transportation	Education & communicatio	Recreation	Tobacco	Restaurant &	Others
US	PCE	17%	33%	5.50%	5%	17.30%	6.70%	8.40%	1.20%	-	6%
UK	CPI	8%	35%	5.70%	2.20%	12.40%	3.80%	12.50%	3.20%	9.80%	7.40%
Japan	CPI	26.20%	33.50%	4.12%	4.30%	14.76% (Trans + Comm)	3.16% (Edu only)	9.89%	-	-	5.70%
Canada	CPI	19.47%	39.90%	5.39%	4.86%	19.72%	10.66% (includes recreation)	-	-	-	-
Australia	CPI	16.10%	31.80%	3.60%	5.40%	10.30%	7%	12.70%	7.10%	-	5.80%
China	CPI	19.90%	28.20%	8%	9.30%	14.5% (Trans + Comm)	8.5% (includes recreation)	-	10.30%	-	1.30%
India	CPI	45.90%	20.80%	6.55%	5.89%	8.59% (Trans +	4.46%	1.68%	2.38%	-	3.89%

Some of the ill-effect of higher inflation in any country:
- Erodes Purchasing power
- Encourages spending rather than saving
- Further inflation loop is created
- Impacts the borrowing rate
- Impacts the exchange rate

Fiscal Policy

Fiscal policy is undertaken by government related to spending and taxing decision. If a government wants to stimulate growth in the economy, it will increase spending for goods and services. This will increase demand for goods and services. When demand goes up, production must go up. If production goes up, companies may need to hire more people. People that were once unemployed may now have jobs and money to spend on goods and services.

This will further increase the demand and require more production and, hopefully, the cycle of growth will continue. Consequently, government spending tends to speed up economic growth.

If the government thinks the economy is overheating – or growing too fast – the government may decrease spending. A decrease in government spending will decrease overall demand in the economy.

Businesses will slow the production, which means profits will decline, resulting in less hiring and business investments.

The other side of fiscal policy is taxes. Decreasing taxes tends to stimulate economic growth. If taxes go down, People will have more money in their pocket. They will either spend it or save it. If they spend it, they increase demand and businesses must produce more. This means they may have to hire more people. These people will then have more money to save or spend. On the other hand, if People save the money, they will put it in the bank. The bank will loan the money they deposited, and borrowers will spend it.

Some economists are concerned that government spending and reduction in taxes will create a crowding out effect. If the government doesn't have enough revenue to support spending, it will have to borrow money. According to some economists, government borrowing tends to increase interest rates. And, increased interest rates discourage individuals and businesses, from borrowing money for spending and investment. According to these economists, government spending may crowd out private investment.

If the government wants to slow down an overheating economy, it may decide to raise taxes. This means people have less money to spend. Fewer people will be hired because there is less demand. Unemployed people don't have extra money to spend. The economy will slow down.

There is an empirical Laffer to show the relationship between tax rate and the amount of tax revenue collected by governments. This relationship is described through the Laffer Curve. It is a theory developed by supply-side economist Arthur. The curve is used to illustrate that sometimes, cut in the tax rates can increase total tax revenue. If taxes are too high, then they will discourage the economic activities, such as work and investment, which leads to reduction in total tax revenue. In this case, cutting tax rates will both stimulate economic incentives and increase tax revenue.

The Laffer Curve

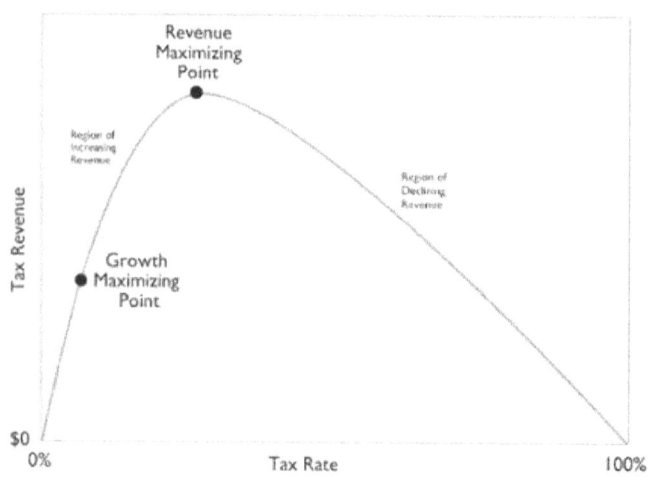

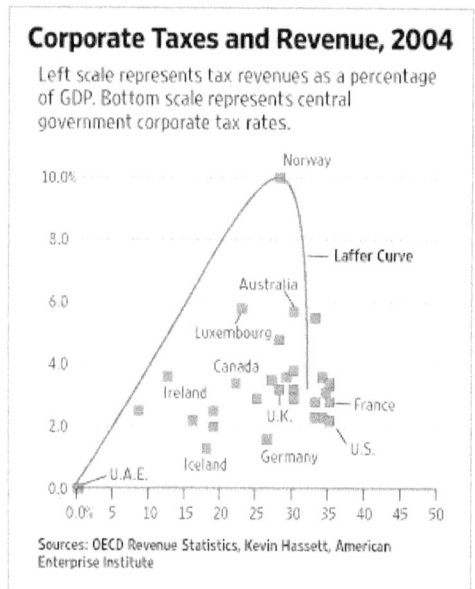

Corporate Taxes and Revenue, 2004

Left scale represents tax revenues as a percentage of GDP. Bottom scale represents central government corporate tax rates.

Sources: OECD Revenue Statistics, Kevin Hassett, American Enterprise Institute

Financial Development

Economic theory suggests that sound and efficient financial systems—banks, equity markets, and bond markets—which channelize capital to its most productive usage are beneficial for economic growth. Sound and efficient financial systems are especially important for sustaining growth in developing economies because efficiency of investment will dictate the growth in these regions, not the quantity of investment.

The efficiency of a financial system is the ability of the system to perform its principal role of transforming deposits to credits. Domestic credit to private sector is usually used as an indicator of financial efficiency.

Domestic credit to private sector (% of GDP) - OECD members, China, India, Sub-Saharan Africa

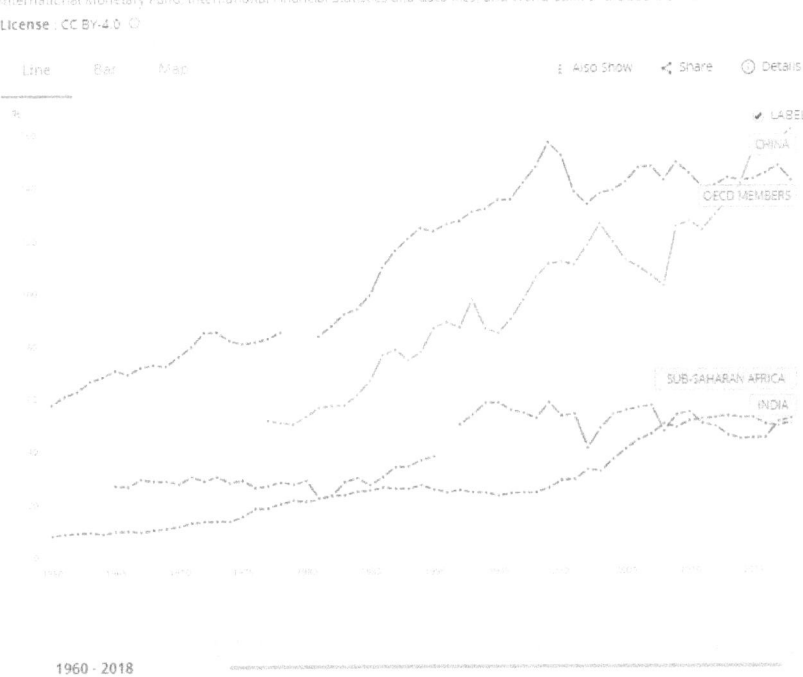

1960 - 2018

Broad money (M2/GDP)

Financial Depth is measured through Broad money in the monetary system. It is expressed as % of GDP.

M2 is a measure of the money supply in the economy that includes cash, checking deposits, and easily convertible near money. M2 is a broader measure of the money supply that includes M1 (which includes cash and checking deposits).

M2 is a closely watched as an indicator of money supply and future inflation and is closely tracked target of central bank monetary policy.

Broad money (% of GDP) - OECD members, China, India, Sub-Saharan Africa (excluding high income)

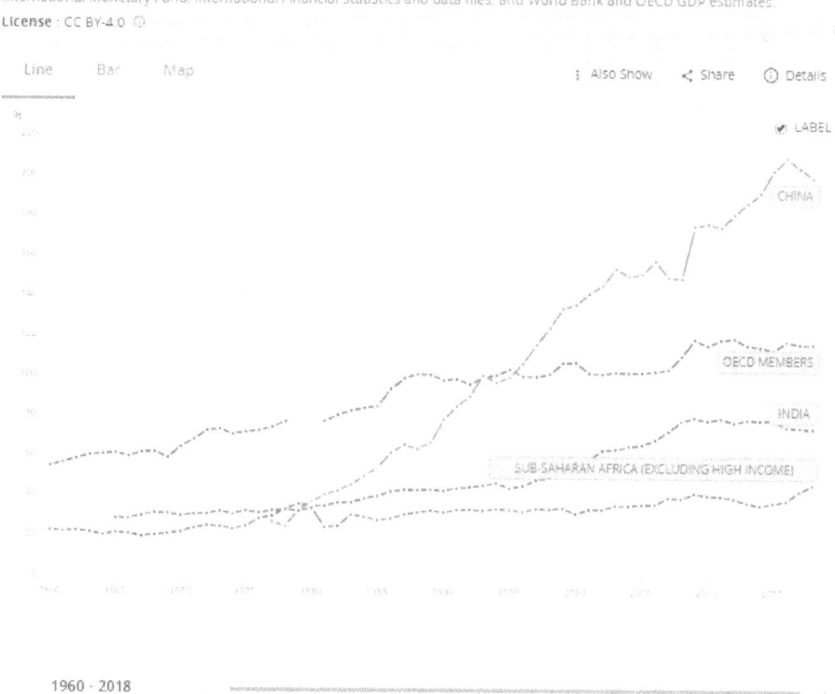

1960 · 2018

Private Investment

It is measured through gross formation of fixed capital (GFCF). It refers to additions of capital goods, such as equipment, tools, transportation assets, and electricity. Countries need capital goods to replace the older ones that are used to produce goods and services. If a country is unable to do so then, the production declines. Usually, the higher the capital formation of an economy, the faster an economy can grow its aggregate income.

If business confidence is low, business houses are less likely to allocate new earnings into additional fixed assets. GFCF is a component of the expenditure measure of GDP (e.g. it represents around 17% of GDP in the UK).

Gross fixed capital formation (% of GDP) - OECD members, China, India, Sub-Saharan Africa

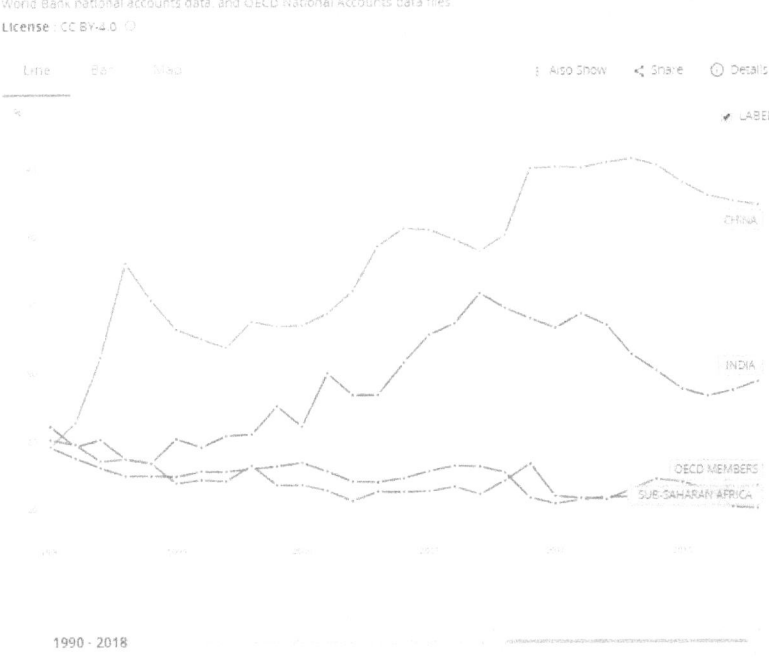

World Bank national accounts data, and OECD National Accounts data files
License : CC BY-4.0

1990 - 2018

International Trade

When the exchange of goods & services takes place across the countries, it is known as International Trade.

Higher the share of trade to country's GDP, the more vulnerable the country is to external economic shocks. In the below chart, it is evident that sub-Saharan African economies have been more dependent on international trade. While, India has been amongst least dependent countries on international trade.

Trade (% of GDP) - OECD members, India, China, Sub-Saharan Africa

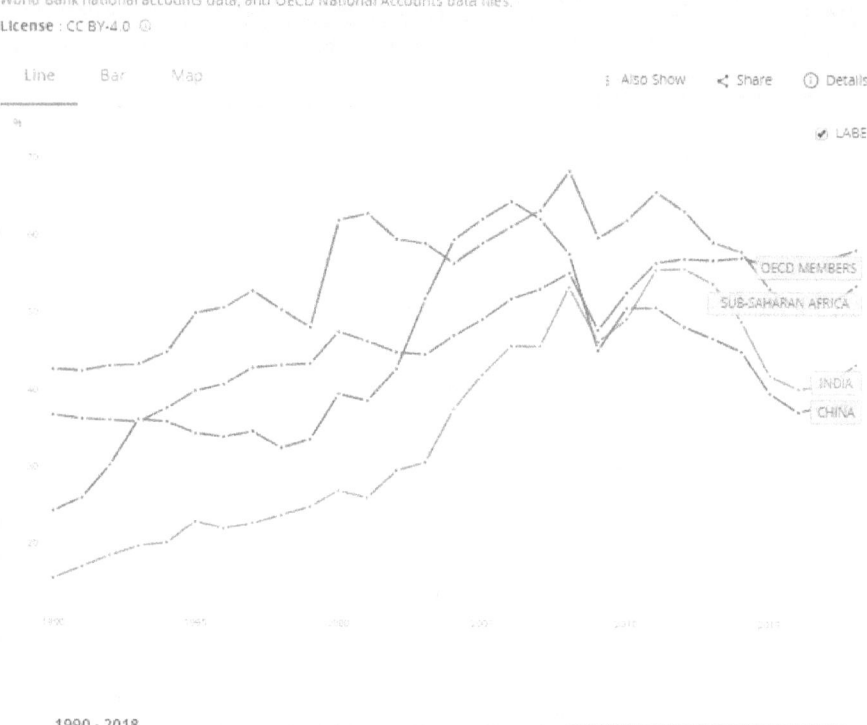

1990 - 2018

Remittances Inflow

Remittances are funds transferred from foreign workers to their home countries. They are the private savings of workers and families that are spent in the home country for food, clothing and other expenditures, and which drive the home country's economy.

Below left-side bar-chart lists the top 10 recipient countries of remittances in US$ terms. The right-side bar-chart lists the top 10 recipient countries of remittances as % of GDP term.

India has been largest recipient of remittances (in dollar terms). China and Mexico are 2nd and 3rd largest recipient of remittances respectively.

Tonga is highest dependent countries in the world on remittance. Haiti and Nepal are 2nd and 3rd most dependent countries respectively.

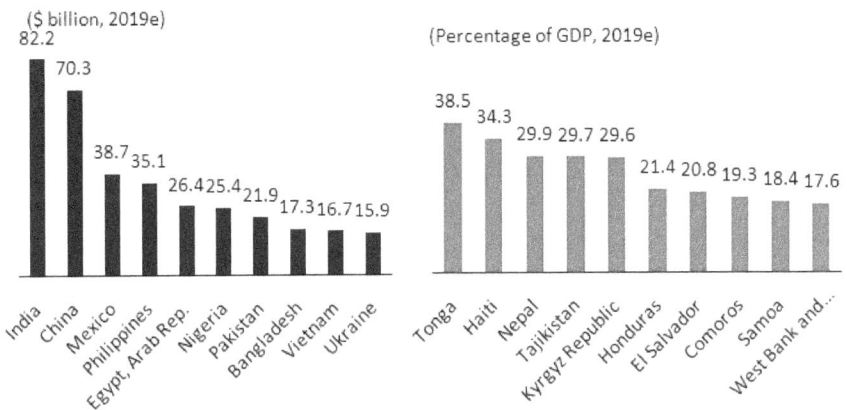

Chapter-6

GDP growth during Unusual Circumstances

- US Growth rate during world war-II
- Nepal Post-Earthquake economic Growth (2015 onwards)
- US GDP growth during 1957 Asian Flu Pandemic

GDP Growth rate, on standalone basis, doesn't tell the whole story about economic well-being of a country. There are many instances when GDP growth rate may be higher because of some special circumstances but would not be sustainable for long time because weaker foundation of economic growth.

US Growth rate during world war-II

World war-II period was one such occasion when US GDP growth was quite higher than usual pre-war period. This world war-II was financed by excessive debt and taxes. Both Personal and gross private domestic investment was at subdued level during 1941-1945.

Government spending, during normal time (prior to WW-II) as % of overall GDP, has remained below the consumer spending. The Government spending was 9.1% of total GDP in 1929 and stable until the U.S. entered WWII. During the period from 1929-1940, government spending averaged 14.2% of total GDP. When the U.S. entered the war, government spending rose sharply, during 1941-1945. It averaged a mammoth 40% of total GDP. Since the end of WWII, it has been stable, averaging close to 20% of total GDP.

Government's consumption increased during this period because of a huge debt and tax collection. Defence spending by government increased manifolds during this period.

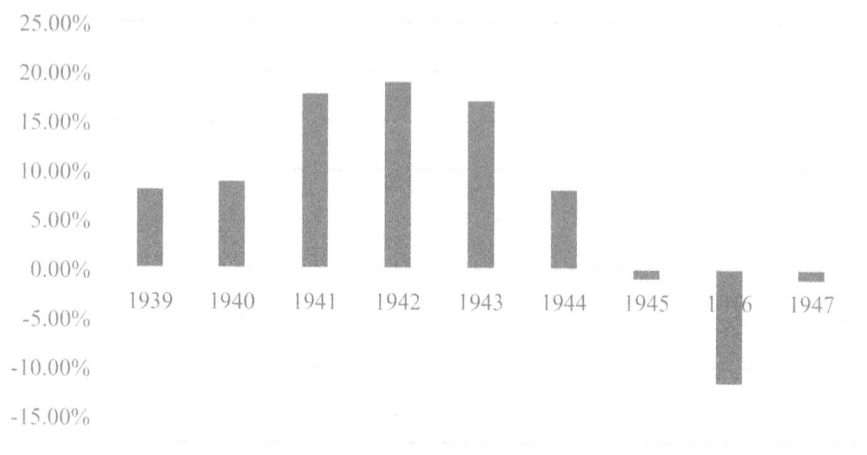

GDP Growth Rate (US) During WW-II

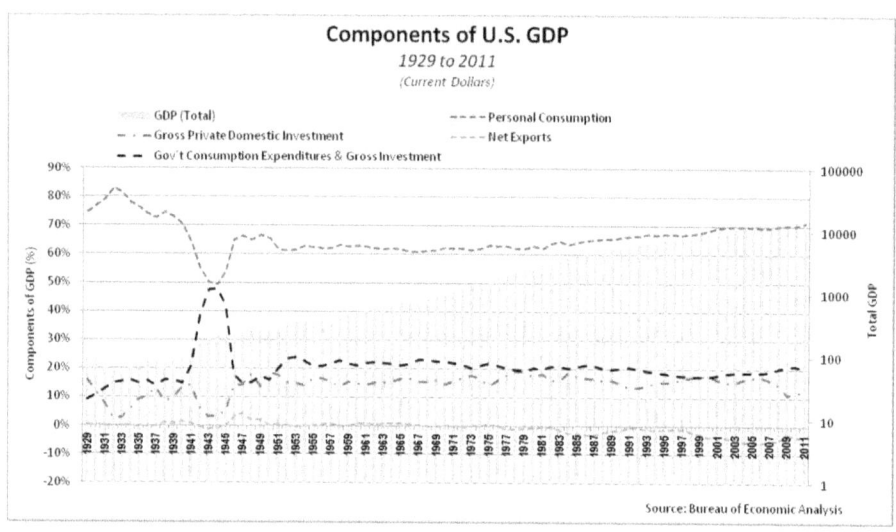

Components of U.S. GDP
1929 to 2011
(Current Dollars)

It resulted in sudden spike in GDP growth rate during this period. Since it was unsustainable growth so it suddenly nosedived once world-war ended in 1945.

Year	GDP Growth Rate	Events
1939	8.00%	WWII, Dust Bowl ended
1940	8.80%	Defence increased
1941	17.70%	Pearl Harbour
1942	18.90%	
1943	17.00%	Defence spending tripled
1944	8.00%	Bretton Woods
1945	-1.00%	WWII ended, recession
1946	-11.60%	Truman budget cuts
1947	-1.10%	Cold War began

Nepal Post-Earthquake economic Growth (2015 onwards)

April 2015 Nepal earthquake killed nearly 9,000 people and injured nearly 22,000. Nepal, with a total GDP of US$20 billion (as per a 2012 estimate), is one of Asia's poorest countries, and has little ability to fund a major reconstruction effort on its own.

Even before the quake, the Asian Development Bank estimated that it would need to spend about four times more than it currently does annually on infrastructure through to 2020 to attract investment. So, earthquake simply aggravated the situation. The U.S. Geological Survey initially estimated economic losses from this calamity at 35-50% of GDP.

There was a sharp drop in GDP growth rate from 6% in 2014 to 3.5% in 2015. It had further lagging effects on the economy in subsequent year as well when economy activities dropped to 0.5% in 2016.

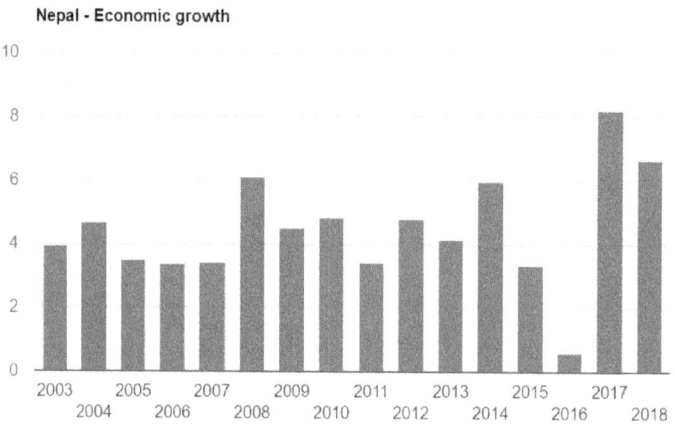

Nepal - Economic growth

Economic growth, that followed in the aftermath of this earthquake, was a sudden spike to 8.2% in 2016 (almost 1.5 year after the earthquake struck the country). This growth rate is unusual growth rate and unlikely to be happen again.

The country needed a huge spending on nation's rebuilding efforts.

Household consumption

Household consumption is that segment of the economy which fluctuates very little in normal economic situation. But consumption was quite uneven in the aftermath of the earthquake. It spiked a little to 80% of total GDP in 2015 from 77.5% in 2014.

A year after, it spiked further to 84% of total GDP. It happened possibly, because of the pent-up demand created from nation rebuilding efforts.

This level of consumption did not sustain for longer periods. Household consumption dropped to 75% of total GDP in 2017. It dropped further to 70% of total GDP in 2018.

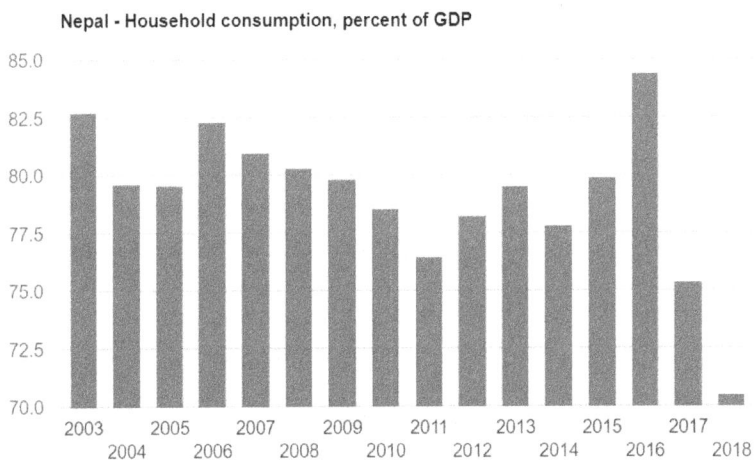

Nepal - Household consumption, percent of GDP

Capital investment

Consumers were the first casualty of the economic malaise created in the aftermath of this earthquake. Then, it spilled over to private enterprise.

Gross Capital formation slowed down from 42% of total GDP in 2014 to 38% of total GDP in 2015. It further dropped to 33% of total GDP in 2016.

In 2017, business sentiments improved, and contribution of capital investment spiked to 47% of total GDP. It went up further to 55% of GDP in 2018.

Nepal - Gross Capital Formation (% Of GDP)

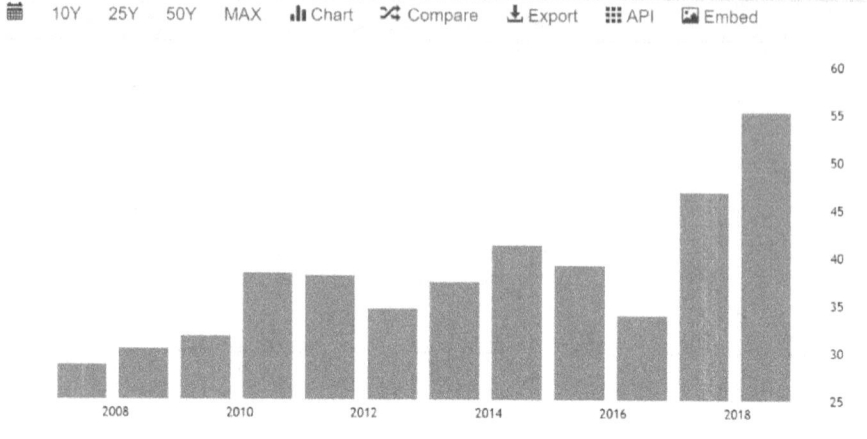

Government Spending

Government spending is very imperative during time of economic crisis. Government usually needs to pull up their socks and increase its spending level. It is often financed through debts, foreign aids, increased taxes.

For a poor country like Nepal, only the first 2 options (Debt and foreign aids) could have been available for adoption by its policy makers.

Government spending increased from 18% of total GDP in 2014 to 20% of total GDP in 2015. It further increased to 22% of total GDP in 2016.

This Government spending level kept on increasing and reached to 32% of total GDP in 2018.

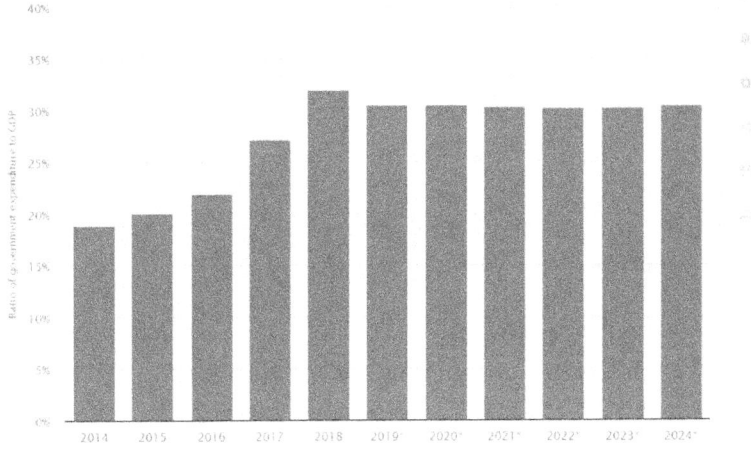

US GDP growth during 1957 Asian Flu Pandemic

Asian Flu Pandemic killed around 70,000 people in US, which seems to be 10% of total fatality of Spanish Flu (in which, almost 700,000 people in US died).

Let's take a look at 1956-1959 quarterly GDP growth rates of US, expressed on year-over-year basis.

Before the Pandemic, the economy was delivering a healthy annualized GDP Growth rate of 2-3%. There was then a sudden slowdown in the second half of 1957 and into early 1958, followed by a strong recovery from Q4 1958 onwards.

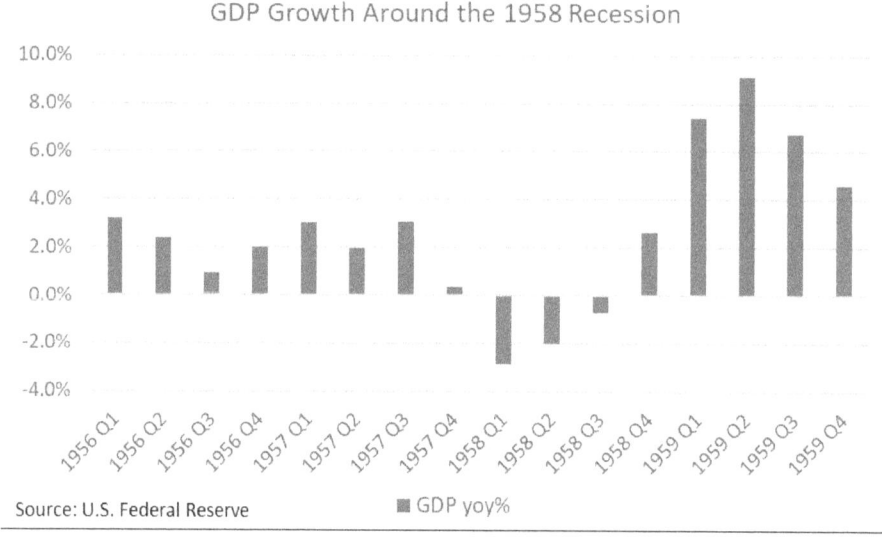

Source: U.S. Federal Reserve

There were 3 quarters of negative growth rates (Q1 1958 to Q3 1958). Though, Q4 1957 was close to zero as well. Then from Q4 1958 onwards, there was a sharp recovery trends in GDP growth rate. GDP growth in Q4 1958 was 2%, it increased to 7.5% in Q1 1959.

It peaked in Q2 1959 at 9%. Such level quarterly growth rate was unprecedented and unsustainable for longer time. It started declining from Q3 1959 onwards to reach at sustainable growth rate of close to 4% level.

Consumer spending trends (as measured by Personal Consumption Expenditures, PCE) reveals that there was just one quarter of negative consumer spending growth (in Q1 1958) during this Pandemic:

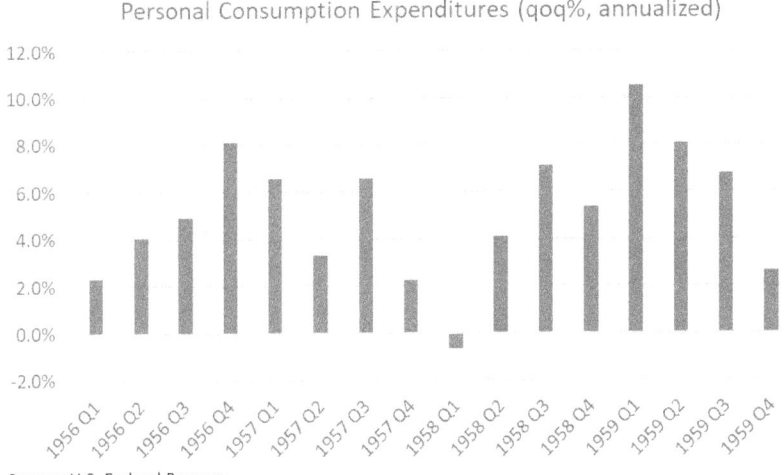

Source: U.S. Federal Reserve

Chapter-7

GDP – Its Limitations and its alternatives

- Arguments against the GDP
- Alternative measures of Socio-economic development
    a. Fordham Index of Social Health (FISH)
    b. Genuine Progress Indicator (GPI)
    c. Human Development Index (HDI)
    d. Happy Planet Index (HPI)

Arguments against the GDP

1. Measures Quantity not Quality

   GDP measures quantity well but it is lousy in measuring the quality. That is the reason that it may not be able to measure the improvement in services industry appropriately (such as improvement in quality of foods, airline's safely records, quality of water supply, etc.).
   Some unfortunate incidents such as plane crash, Industrial disaster (e.g. Bhopal gas accident) or earthquake can raise the GDP figure through rebuilding efforts without any adequate incremental development.

   GDP includes cars built, concerts done by Lady Gaga and broadband connections made – which seems just fine. But it also counts plastic waste floating in the ocean, financial speculations and petrol consumed while stuck in a traffic.
   Pragmatically speaking, the items which are detrimental for human lives or environment ought to be subtracted, not added.

2. Fails to Measure Productivity

   GDP does not measure the efficiency or productivity of the nation. Internet and telecommunication system have evolved leaps & bounds during past few decades. But this efficiency has been achieved by getting rid of unproductive manual workforce. GDP will go down because it has forced many unproductive people out of the employment because this efficiency.

3. Disregards Inequality

   GDP disregards the distribution of wealth or inequality. Statistics such as GDP per capita, supposedly, a proxy for measuring how wealthy the residents of a country are, is an average figure. An average figure does not reflect the true picture of the distribution of wealth among the people.

   A median would have been a tad better than mean figure. Distribution of income is skewed in most of the countries.

So, an increase in income of top 5% people (who controls 2/3rd of the income) can lead to significant increase in GDP per capita of whole nation. It won't tell a true story about remaining 95% of population (who control 1/3rd of the nation's income).

4. Leads to Misplaced Priorities

GDP measurement gives rise to skewed priorities to the Government. It measures a nuclear warhead same as a new hospital beds or a new school.
When GDP was first adopted, it was quite well-understood that it has nothing to do with well-being. But too often we confuse the two.

Across the world, we have developed an obsession with fast economic growth. It has been considered a mark of success, no matter at what expense that growth is coming. Because of this obsession with a higher growth rate, if something has to be sacrificed (e.g. clean air, public services, or equality of opportunity) to get the GDP growth then we are ready to do so, without a second-thought.

5. Informal Sector is overlooked

It excludes the income of informal sectors, which forms a significant portion of developing country's economy. Global average of informal segment of employment is around 60% of total employment. For India, it forms almost 80% of total employment.
Some of those informal sector activities are babysitting, lawn mowing and other grey or black markets transactions. These informal sector activities remain unreported in country's overall output or GDP.

6. Nation's wealth is Overlooked

It fails to measure the wealth of a country. It only measures the annual income, that too, is backward looking. It fails to predict the income in the following year. If we compare a nation's economic scorecard with a company's scorecard then we will find that company prepares both Income statement (for past year's performance) and Balance sheet statement (as of date, wealth and liabilities).

Balance sheet forms the basis for the company for predicting the future's income estimates. Similar Balance sheet for a nation's economic wealth and liability is not available to predict its future income estimates.

A historic average GDP growth rate may not be a correct way to predict the future GDP growth rate as economic factors that facilitated the growth in the past may no longer be favourable anymore.

7. Nation's Debt is Incorrectly measured

Nation's Debt is usually measured inappropriately as Debt-to-GDP ratio. But as we know that not the country's entire GDP (which is also understood as "National Income") is available to the government as tax revenue. Government has resources in terms of its direct and indirect tax collections only.

So, a higher GDP does not necessarily mean than the country has a higher capacity to repay the debt.
A better comparison will be to examine each country's debt to government tax revenue, since that is the government's income. This is also a comparative ratio as different countries have very a different level of taxation.

A country with high taxes can afford more debt than a low tax country. Debt to GDP disregards this difference. Comparing debt to tax revenue provides a much clearer picture of the burden of each country's debt on its government's finances.

e.g. When we use "debt to tax revenue ratio" to compare the country's ranking then the US jumps up to 3rd place (in OECD countries). But US is at a distant 11th place when Debt-to-GDP ratio is used.

8. Fails to measure the sustainability aspects

A measurement that measures the growth of economic activities must be sustainable enough, for it to be reliable. GDP fails on that account. It fails to subtract the depletion of natural resources or exploitation of environment or carbon emission generated from overall growth figure.

9. Fails to measure depreciation of capital stocks

Though GDP measures the investment in new green-field projects (i.e. new capital) but it fails to subtract depleted value of depreciated capital stocks (e.g. plant, equipment, and other assets that help with production).

10. Higher GDP per capita not an indicator of prosperity

Below is equilibrium curve line of country having people living a content life as well as having a higher GDP per capita, for OECD and non-OECD countries.
- There are countries who find their place above this curve but its GDP per capita is not that higher. e.g. Mexico, Vietnam, China, etc.
- There are countries who stand below this curve but have a higher GDP per capita. e.g. Australia, Singapore, France, US, etc.
- There are countries who are blessed with both – higher GDP per capita as well as higher happiness level. e.g. Finland, Sweden, Netherlands, etc.
- There are few countries who are neither blessed with higher GDP per capita nor happiness level. They score low on both counts. e.g. India, Iraq, Egypt, etc.

Happiness and income per capita

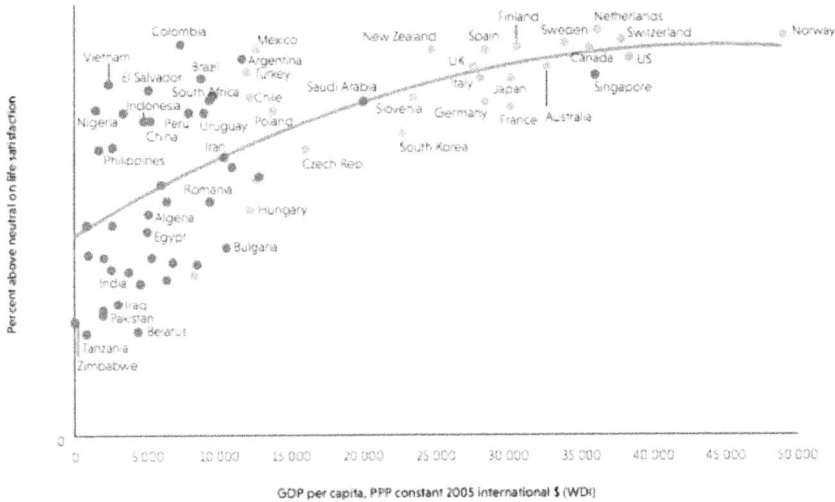

Alternative measures of Socio-economic development

We know a lot more about GDP now. Let's take a look at other alternative measures which can be used along with GDP to overcome the shortcomings of GDP. These measures act may prove to be a complementary to GDP.

Fordham Index of Social Health (FISH)

The Fordham Institute for Innovation in Social Policy came up with the social health index as measure of the social prosperity, especially of the American society. The Social Health Index has been released every year since 1987. Just like GDP and other economic indicators, the Index of Social Health is determined and released every year to give a preview of the social wellbeing of a country.

Taking the United States as an example, despite the economic recession ending in 2009, the Index of Social Health has remained low. While the GDP continues to grow in aftermath of the economic recession, social indicators (e.g. quality of life) remain low. It infers that the individual has not yet felt the requisite change occasioned by the economic recovery as shown by the GDP.

While some indicators in the Index of Social Health have improved, some have experienced either slow or lack of progress. A good example are the United States and Canada, where while the GDP has increased, the Social Health Index has remained constant in Canada and declined in the United States since 1973. Below is the list of segments included in FISH.

	FISH
infant mortality	*
child abuse	*
child/elderly poverty	*
teen suicide	*
drug abuse	*
high school drop outs	*
unemployment and underemployment	*
health insurance coverage	*
highway deaths due to alcohol	*
homicides/crime	*
food stamp distribution	*
housing	*
income inequality/distribution	*

Genuine Progress Indicator (GPI)

Genuine progress indicator (GPI) is a metric that can replace, or supplement, GDP. The GPI is designed to take fuller account of the well-being of a nation, size of the nation's economy is one of the several factors that is considered for this metric.

It also incorporates the environmental and social factors, which are not measured by GDP. For instance, some models of GPI decrease in value when the poverty rate increases. The GPI separates the concept of societal progress from economic growth.

GPI is thought to be a better measure of the sustainability of an economy vis-a-vis the GDP measure. Since 1995, the adoption of GPI indicator has increased and is used in Canada and the United States. though, both these countries still report their economic performance in GDP terms as well in order to remain aligned with the other countries.

GPI is calculated using below simple equation:

$$GPI = A + B - C - D + I$$

- A is income weighted private consumption
- B is value of non-market services generating welfare
- C is private defensive cost of natural deterioration
- D is cost of deterioration of nature and natural resources
- I is increase in capital stock and balance of international trade

The GPI indicator is based on the concept of sustainable income, espoused by economist John Hicks (1948). The sustainable income is the amount a person or an economy can consume during one period without decreasing his or her consumption during the next period. In the same manner, GPI depicts the state of welfare in the society by taking into account the ability to maintain welfare on at least the same level in the future.

Below chart shows the relationship between GDP per capita and GPI per capita for US economy. It shows that as GDP per capita has been rising over past 44 years, GPI per capita (i.e. indicator of progress) has remained at the same level during the same period.

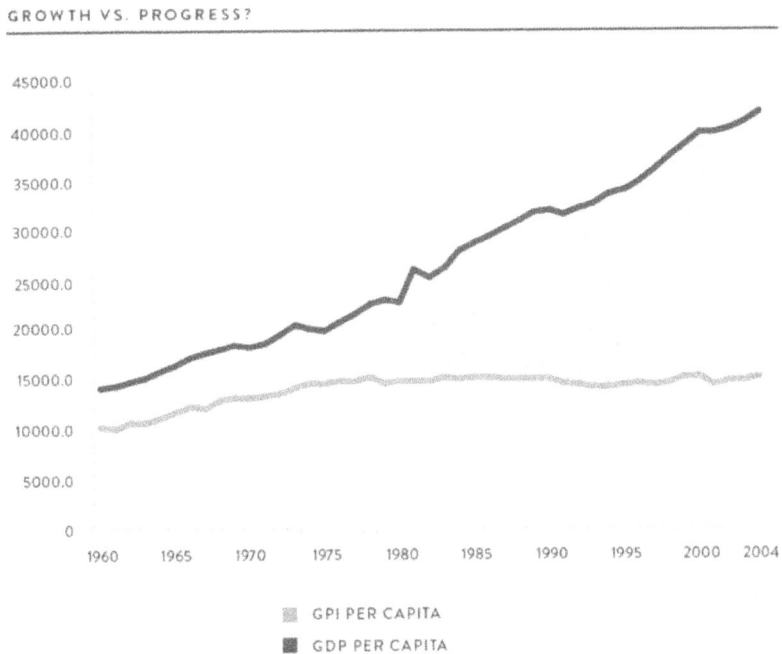

GPI PER CAPITA
GDP PER CAPITA

How GPI is different from GDP?

GDP increases on two occasions – 1. when pollution is created (as a side-effect of some costlier industrial process) and 2. when the pollution is cleaned up.

On the contrary, GPI counts the initial pollution as a loss, not a gain, equal to the amount it will cost to clean up later plus the cost of any negative impact the pollution will have in the meantime.

The relationship between GDP and GPI is quite like what we have between the gross profit and net profit of a company.

The net profit is the gross profit minus the costs incurred, while the GPI is the GDP (value of all goods and services produced) minus the environmental and social costs. Going by this principle, the GPI will be zero if the financial costs of poverty and pollution equal the financial gains in production of goods and services.

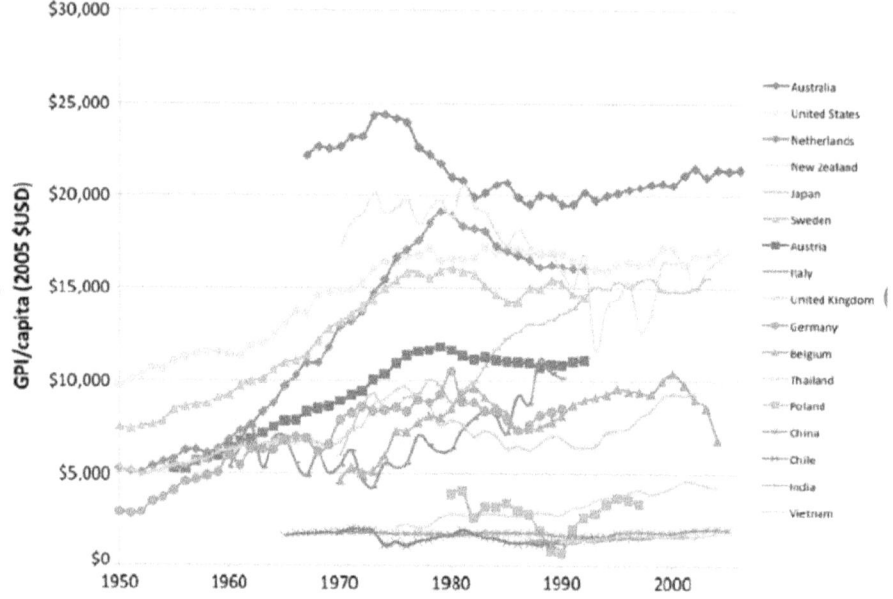

Human Development Index (HDI)

HDI has been conceptualised to measure human and economic development of a country. It is based on three important dimensions:

<u>Healthy and long life</u>

It is measured by life expectancy of people at birth. Its index is called "Life Expectancy Index" (LEI). LEI is 1, when Life expectancy at birth is 85 and LEI is 0, when Life expectancy at birth is 20. African countries where life expectancy is abysmally low (close to 50 years), LEI is 0.5.

<u>Access to Education</u>

There are two levels of measurement to measure the access to education:

a. Expected years of schooling of children at school-entry age level (Index Name is EYSI). EYSI is 1, if expected years of schooling is 18 (this period is equivalent to acquiring a master's degree).
b. Mean years of schooling of the adult population (Index name is MYSI). MYSI is 1, if mean years of schooling is 15.

Access to Education is compared across the countries by using an index named "Education Index" (EI). It is the mean of EYSI and MYSI index value.

<u>Better Standard of living</u>

It is measured by Gross national product (GNP) per capita in purchasing power parity (PPP, US$) term. So, if a country wants to see higher HDI Index value then it needs to score higher on all 3 parameters - life expectancy, education and GNP per capita.

It was envisioned by two economists – Mahmub-ul-Haq and Amartya Sen. Later, it was adopted by United Nations Development Programme (UNDP) in 2010. Its index is called "Income Index" (II). Income Index (II) is 1, when GNI per capita is $75,000 and Income Index (II) is 0, when GNI per capita is $100.

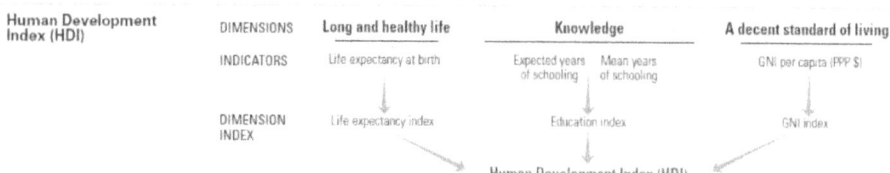

HDI is finally computed by taking the Geometric mean of above three indices – LEI, EI, II.

HDI = (LEI x EI x II) ^ (1/3).

Below are the top 10 countries as per 2018 Human Development Index (HDI) –

HDI Rank	Country	HDI Index	Change Vs Previous year
1	Norway	0.954	0.001
2	Switzerland	0.946	0.003
3	Ireland	0.942	0.003
4	Germany	0.939	0.001
4	Hong Kong	0.939	0.003
6	Iceland	0.938	0.003
6	Australia	0.938	0.001
8	Sweden	0.937	0.001
9	Singapore	0.935	0.001
10	Netherlands	0.933	0.001

The bottom HDI ranks are taken by African countries such as Niger, Ethiopia, Congo republic, Chad to name a few.

Happy Planet Index (HPI)

Happy Planet Index measures sustainable well being of the people living within a country. Wealthy western countries (with high per capita income) usually scores low on the HPI. Many countries from Latin America and Asia Pacific scores high on HPI because of higher life expectancy and lower carbon emission level.

The objective of this index is to propagate a message that it is feasible to live better lives without destructing the nature.

It measures 4 dimensions of the development –

Well-being

It measures the overall level of satisfaction of people with their respective lives. It is computed by conducting "Gallup World Poll". This poll is a set of 100 global questions and a few regions specific items. Gallup asks people from Brazil to Bangladesh the same questions, every year, in the same way. This makes it possible to trend data from year to year and make direct country comparisons.

The question that is used a part of the survey is also known as the Cantril Self-Anchoring Scale or the Ladder of Life. It has been used in surveys since the 1960s, and its validity has been demonstrated in a range of different contexts around the world.

Life Expectancy

It measures the average number of years a person is expected to live(life-span) in a country. It is based on data collected by UN.

Inequality of outcomes

It measures inequalities in the data – Well-being and Life Expectancy between people within a country. It is expressed as percentage.

Ecological Footprints

It measures the average impact that people place on the environment. It is computed by Global Footprint Network. It is expressed as global hectares (GHA) per person.

HPI data is not available for all the countries. The data for above 3 dimensions has been sourced from the United Nations, Gallup World Poll and the Global Footprint Network to calculate the Happy Planet Index score for each individual country.

The top 10 highest scoring happiest countries in the world are (in alphabetical order):

- Belize
- Colombia
- Costa Rica
- El Salvador
- Guatemala
- Jamaica
- Nicaragua
- Panama
- Venezuela
- Vietnam

These countries made it to the list of the top due to scoring higher on life expectancy and environmental impact, meaning that these are the most sustainable countries, even though they suffer through high levels of poverty.

The lowest 10 scoring countries (less happiest countries) in the world are:

- Bahrain
- Botswana
- Chad
- Central African Republic

- Kuwait
- Mali
- Mongolia
- Niger
- South Africa
- Qatar

These lowest ranking 10 countries are probably expected to have higher rankings however their environmental footprint lets them down immensely.

Chapter-8

GDP - Myths Associated with it

- Myth-1: High GDP growth is positively correlated with Personal Income
- Myth-2: GDP of a country is comparable to Market Cap of a Company
- Myth-3: Debt-to-GDP, not Debt-to-Revenue, is a better measure of credit worthiness of a country

Myth-1: High GDP growth is positively correlated with Personal Income

As a country witnesses a steady growth in its economic activities, the country becomes the growth driver of the entire world. But growth in economic activities may not always translate into similar growth in country's other metrics of social progress. GDP growth may translate into higher GDP per capita value, but it does not translate into higher median personal income for majority of residents of the country. It is because of growing inequality in the society as country witnesses an increase in its economic activities.

Below graph displays the 30 years history of GDP growth rate Vs growth of median individual income of US. It shows that the median individual income over 30 years period has remained almost unchanged, while GDP per capita has increased more than 2-times over the period.

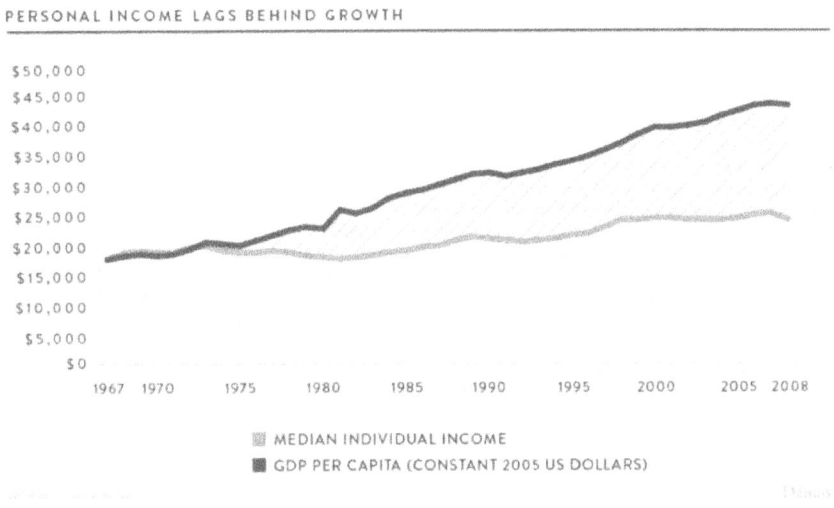

The sole reason, for the incoherence is, an increase in income inequality in the society. In the below chart, we have used "GINI Coefficient" to measure the income inequality. The Gini coefficient, which is also known as "Gini index" or "Gini ratio", is a measure of dispersion. It represents the income or wealth distribution of residents of a country and is the most widely used measurement of inequality.

We can see in below graph that with a rise in US GDP (economy size), the income inequality has also been rising.

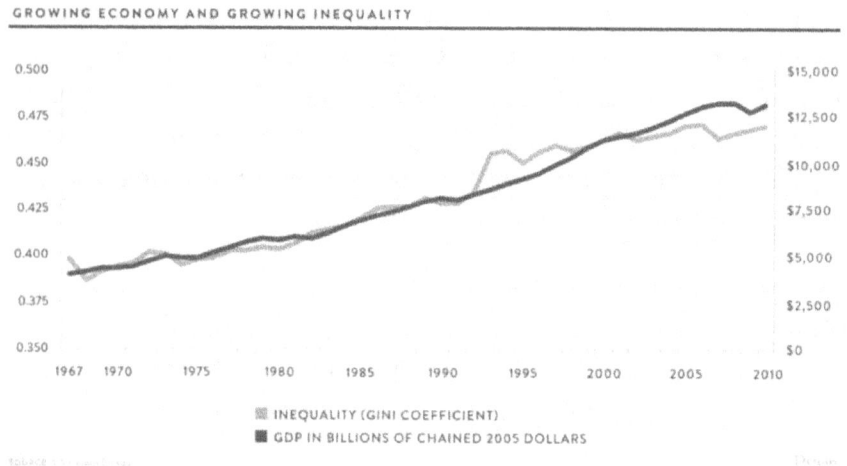

INEQUALITY (GINI COEFFICIENT)
GDP IN BILLIONS OF CHAINED 2005 DOLLARS

Myth-2: GDP of a country is comparable to Market Cap of a Company

Of late, we witnessed around 6 instances when the market capitalisation of a publicly listed company surpassed the symbolic milestone of $1 trillion valuation.

PetroChina was the first company to achieve this coveted feat. It did it in 2007. Apple and Amazon registered their name to this $1 trillion market capitalisation club (in August and September 2018 respectively). Then Microsoft achieved it in June 2019. Saudi Aramco did it after listing its share in Dec 2019. The latest company to enter this club is Alphabet, who did it in Jan 2020.

There is some new trend emerging in some section of business and mainstream media to compare the GDP of country with Market capitalisation of a listed company (mostly the $1 trillion club companies).

Such loose comparison disregards the difference between the value of an asset with the amount of money generated or spent over time. One might earn huge amounts of money, but if he/she overspends, or take on too much debts, he/she can still be poor. Just take the example of Pirates of Caribbean actor Johnny Depp. Income or earnings is like a cashflow. Wealth is a stock.

Comparing GDP with Market capitalisation of a listed company is akin to comparing Income with Wealth. Both are not comparable to each other.

When Apple had entered the $1 trillion-dollar club in 2018, then it was reported by some section of media that Apple's market value would rank No. 17 in the list of top countries by GDP, if it was a country. Apple will be just behind Indonesia, with its $1.07 trillion GDP. But such reporting is quite a mischievous act.

It would be more apt if we do a comparison between Apple's revenue and Indonesia's GDP, because GDP, per se, is not a measure of wealth but rather it's a measure of output: the total value of goods and services produced by the country in a year. Apple's total revenue (Gross) in 2018 was $265 billion—a huge figure, but it was just close to 25% of the company's market cap and Indonesia's GDP.

Likewise, Indonesia's market value is not its GDP but rather it is the sum of all assets in the country, which is going to be enormously larger than Apple's market value.

Myth-3: Debt-to-GDP, not Debt-to-Revenue, is a better measure of credit worthiness of a country

Measuring a country's debt as a percent of GDP may be a common international norm, but it makes little sense since GDP is equivalent to country's revenue collection. i.e. not all national income is collected in taxes. Debt to government tax revenue is more sensible approach to gauge the level of debt that a country has taken.

When we express the debt in terms of country's GDP then the idea is to compare how much a country owes to how much it earns (since GDP is understood to be the national income). The problem with this idea is that it is irrational. The government does not have access to country's GDP i.e. national income, only the portion of national income that it collects as taxes are available to government as revenue.

The country's debt to government tax revenue offers a better comparison because different countries have very different levels of taxation. A country with high taxes can afford more debts than a country with low taxation rate. Debt to GDP ignores this difference. Comparing debt to tax revenue reveals a much truer picture of the burden of each country's debt on its government's finances.

If we use Debt to government tax revenue and rank the country then Japan is still #1, with a debt as a percentage of tax revenue and Greece is still in second place. The big change is the U.S. jumps up to third place.

References:

https://economictimes.indiatimes.com/articleshow/70916309.cms?
from=mdr&utm_source=contentofinterest&utm_medium=text&ut
m_campaign=cppst

https://en.wikipedia.org/wiki/Human_Development_Index

https://www.foreignaffairs.com/reviews/capsule-review/2016-08-
10/power-single-number-political-history-gdp-great-invention-story

https://www.theglobalist.com/warfare-and-the-invention-of-gdp/

https://www.oecd.org/

http://www.nber.org/papers/w3899

https://foreignpolicy.com/2011/01/03/gdp-a-brief-history/

http://www.oecd.org/economy/growth/18450995.pdf

https://www.nationsencyclopedia.com/Americas/Brazil-PUBLIC-
FINANCE.html

https://www.theglobaleconomy.com/

http://globalcommunitywebnet.com/globalcommunity/measureme
ntofsd.htm

https://www.visualcapitalist.com/american-income-levels-by-age-
group/

https://www.demos.org/research/does-growth-equal-progress-
myth-gdp